THE ATLANTIC CRITICAL STUDIES

WILLIAM SHAKESPEARE'S

Macbeth

RATRI RAY

Published by

PUBLISHERS & DISTRIBUTORS (P) LTD
7/22, Ansari Road, Darya Ganj, New Delhi-110002
Phones : +91-11-40775252, 40775214, 23273880, 23275880
Fax : +91-11-23285873
Web : www.atlanticbooks.com
E-mail : orders@atlanticbooks.com

Branch Office
5, Nallathambi Street, Wallajah Road, Chennai-600002
Phones : +91-44-48531784, 28411383
E-mail : chennai@atlanticbooks.com

Printed in India at Nice Printing Press, A-33/3A, Site-IV, Industrial Area, Sahibabad, Ghaziabad, U.P.

General Preface

The study-aids available in England and America, among other places, form the basis of *The Atlantic Critical Studies* which is primarily meant to cater to the needs of the students of English literature in Indian universities.

The students in India pursuing English Honours and postgraduation in English have to study under various constraints like non-availability of relevant critical books, dearth of foreign and Indian journals, inaccessibility to good and well-equipped libraries, among others. Although Internet is of great help to the students these days, yet the plethora of information it brings before them often confuses them and they end up choosing a lot of irrelevant material which shifts the focus away from the topic or theme under discussion.

The books under *The Atlantic Critical Studies* fill the gap between the requirements and availability, and help the students by providing them quality material pertinent to their academic pursuits.

The series covers authors and works that are widely prescribed in Indian universities. This was necessary considering a regular demand for books that critically examine these authors and their works. The books in the series discuss all the major aspects of the works, besides providing sufficient information on the authors and the period in which they wrote. This makes each book in the series self-sufficient and of great benefit to the students. The scholarly authors who have prepared the books in the series have used authentic sources and taken special care to combine lucidity and profundity in their treatment of the texts.

The References in each chapter and the Select Bibliography at the end of the book are meant to help the students in making further study in specific areas if they want to.

The books in *The Atlantic Critical Studies* will also help researchers besides students and teachers of English literature.

Ratri Ray

Preface

Macbeth is one of the masterpieces of Shakespeare and he himself is definitely the brightest star in the galaxy of Elizabethan writers. He is the brightest star in every field, whether tragedy, comedy, narrative poetry, or sonneteering. That is why, referring to him, Matthew Arnold had said: "Others abide our question, Thou art free". That is to say, Shakespeare's supremacy is beyond our questions or doubts.

Shakespeare's plays are divided into several groups and that of the Four Great Tragedies is one of them. *Macbeth* belongs to this group. It is definitely one of his maturest plays. Not only does it satisfy all the rules and conventions prevalent at that time, but also, as is so often the case with Shakespeare, soars above the other tragedies of this kind. It is a conqueror tragedy, but it is much more than merely such. As is usual with him, Shakespeare uses the form as a springboard to soar up into literary and psychological heights where no one can follow him. The diligent student will discover in the following pages, that this is no idle claim.

A filling socio-political as well as literary background has been provided along with chronological tables without which no such study can be complete. After this, every possible aspect of the play has been studied in detail, with copious quotations from, and opinions of, other critics. No study of Shakespeare can be at all effective unless other critical opinions are consulted and these have been abundantly provided in the book. The play was written in honour of King James, who was Scottish just as Macbeth was.

Ratri Ray

The Atlantic Critical Studies

D.H. Lawrence's ***Sons and Lovers*** by *Atlantic Research Division*, pp. 168, ₹ 495.00

E.M. Forster's ***A Passage to India*** by *Rama Kundu*, pp. 296, 2007, ₹ 550.00

Emily Brontë's ***Wuthering Heights*** by *Jibesh Bhattacharyya*, pp. 192, ₹ 350.00

Ernest Hemingway's ***A Farewell to Arms*** by *P.G. Rama Rao*, pp. 168, ₹ 350.00

Ernest Hemingway's ***The Old Man and the Sea*** by *P.G. Rama Rao*, pp. 160, ₹ 395.00

Jane Austen's ***Pride and Prejudice*** by *Jibesh Bhattacharyya*, pp. 192, ₹ 350.00

Joseph Conrad's ***Heart of Darkness*** by *Mohit Kumar Ray*, pp. 208, ₹ 495.00

Ruth Prawer Jhabvala's ***Heat and Dust*** by *I.H. Shihan*, pp. 160, ₹ 350.00

Salman Rushdie's ***Midnight's Children*** by *Pradip Kumar Dey*, pp. 168, ₹ 395.00

William Golding's ***Lord of the Flies*** by *Santwana Haldar*, pp. 184, ₹ 495.00

William Shakespeare's ***Antony and Cleopatra*** by *Ratri Ray*, pp. 208, ₹ 495.00

William Shakespeare's ***Othello*** by *Jibesh Bhattacharyya*, pp. 232, ₹ 450.00

William Shakespeare's ***The Merchant of Venice*** by *Ratri Ray*, pp. 184, ₹ 375.00

William Shakespeare's ***A Midsummer Night's Dream*** by *Ratri Ray*, pp. 192, ₹ 395.00

William Shakespeare's ***As You Like It*** *by Ratri Ray*, pp. 200, ₹ 450.00

William Shakespeare's ***Hamlet*** by *Ratri Ray*, pp. 216, ₹ 495.00

William Shakespeare's ***Julius Caesar*** by *Ratri Ray*, pp. 200, ₹ 495.00

William Shakespeare's ***King Lear*** by *Ratri Ray*, pp. 184, ₹ 395.00

William Shakespeare's ***Othello*** by *Ratri Ray*, pp. 208, ₹ 395.00

William Shakespeare's ***The Tempest*** by *Ratri Ray*, pp. 192, ₹ 395.00

William Shakespeare's ***Twelfth Night*** by *Ratri Ray*, pp. 224, ₹ 395.00

Introduction

The present work is limited to the study of one of Shakespeare's plays, but the student should know that the multifariousness of Shakespeare's genius is really awesome. This is the feature that made Dr. Johnson say that whereas a diligent and careful writer might produce what might be called a well-planned garden, Shakespeare is a whole forest unto himself.[1] He alone, in the galaxy of Elizabethan poets and dramatists, used many different literary forms and excelled in each of them so that they have become ideal examples—matter for study and emulation. But he was no dreamer in an ivory tower. He was a very practical man with a hard-headed sense of real life, which made him one of the richest men of his village. When he retired from the stage, he had come to own a large share in the theatrical company in which he acted, had become one of the most honoured families in the village by climbing up the social ladder into the class of landed gentry with his own coat of arms. This makes one wonder at the creative genius he was. Indeed, genius is the only word to be used—a man of a different category from others, a man not to be questioned but marveled at. Matthew Arnold rightly says:

> Others abide our question. Thou art free.[2]

Shakespeare had about two decades of creative activity and within these twenty years he poured out, in all, thirty-seven plays, a hundred and fifty-four sonnets, three narrative poems and numerous songs. In each of them he attained perfection. Each of the forms had certain rules concerned with it—classical or Elizabethan. With the sovereign assurance of a master, he observed them when it suited him and neglected them when they impeded him. As shall be seen in the following chapters, the different elements of a play, character, plot, style, etc., had all reached such a harmonious excellence in his plays that most of the time rules did not matter at all. Critics belonging to many different schools of criticism have taken up his works as a challenge but none has succeeded in exhausting the possibilities inherent in his works. In the four or more centuries after his death criticism has been enriched by his works so that a study of Shakespeare criticism is itself a complex matter. Some hint of this will be given in Chapter 11 of the present work.

Shakespeare wrote different varieties of tragedies, comedies and histories which no other playwright of his time did. Marlowe, for example, wrote only tragedies and Ben Jonson only comedies and that too of one variety only. Since the work under discussion is a tragedy, let us take this genre only. There were four kinds of tragedies at that time and he has written all of them. The work for discussion is a conqueror tragedy like those of Marlowe, *Hamlet* is a revenge tragedy, *Othello* a villain tragedy and *Romeo and Juliet* a domestic one, whereas *King Lear* defies all classifications. Let it be remembered that all these labels are given only for the sake of convenience. The plays are much more than these tags can suggest. Moreover the same play can cover more than one category. *Othello*, for example, has been called, with equal justification, a villain tragedy as well as a domestic tragedy.

A classification of Shakespeare's tragedies has been made according to chronology. Again, these periods and the classification itself, are flexible. They frequently overlap, let the student remember.

The Early Tragedies: *Titus Andronicus*, *Romeo and Juliet*.

The Four Great Tragedies: *Hamlet*, *Othello*, *King Lear*, *Macbeth*.

The Roman Tragedies: *Julius Caesar*, *Antony and Cleopatra*, *Coriolanus*.

It is a well-known fact that parallels have been drawn between Shaw and Shakespeare. Yet Shaw himself had never been at all under any illusion about it. He had said:

> As far as sonority, imagery, wit, humour, energy of imagination, power over language and a keen eye for idiosyncrasies can make a dramatist, Shakespeare was the king of dramatists.[3]

NOTES

1. Frank Brady and W.K. Wimsatt ed., *Samuel Johnson: Selected Poetry and Prose*. University of California, Press, 1975. p. 316.
2. Mathew Arnold, *Shakespeare, The Golden Treasury*, ed. by Palgrave, London, OUP, 1960, p. 419.
3. Shaw, *Saturday Review*, 29 Jan. 1888. Quoted in Ure, P. ed., *Julius Caesar: A Case-book*, Macmillan, London, 1969, p. 40.

Contents

1

The Background

(A) THE SOCIO-POLITICAL BACKGROUND

A writer, dramatist or poet can never be separated from his background. Even if he sets himself against society and rebels from it, even then he is related to it as a rebel. A chronological table of the most important political and social events of Shakespeare's time is given below. It starts a few years before his birth and ends with his death. His own works have not been mentioned which come later (*vide* chap. 2 *infra*).

A Chronological Table

1558 – Queen Mary I dies. Elizabeth I succeeds.
– Mary Queen of Scots marries the French Dauphin.
– The French capture Calais.

'59 – Mary Queen of Scots declares herself the Queen of England in spite of Elizabeth.
– War between Spain and France ends.
– Church of England re-established more firmly.

'60 – The Scottish Parliament establishes the Reformed Church and breaks with Rome and the Pope.
– Mary Queen of Scots returns from France.
– She clashes with the calvinists.

'62 – The Huguenot settlers emigrate from France to England.

'63 – Bubonic plague in Europe.

'64 – Shakespeare born. Galileo born.
– England at war with Spain.
– The Thirty-nine Articles adopted by the Church of England. Queen Elizabeth makes a laudable attempt at enforcing uniformity of religion.

1567 – Mary Queen of Scots abdicates.
– Rugby Chapel founded.
'68 – Mary Queen of Scots flees to England. She is imprisoned by Queen Elizabeth.
'69 – Rebellion of Roman Catholic earls crushed.
'70 – Pope Pius V excommunicates Elizabeth.
'74 – Burbage gets license to build the first theatre in London.
'76 – Tycho Brahe begins his astronomical observations.
– Burbage opens the first theatre in London at Shoreditch.
'77 – England makes a treaty with the Dutch.
Sir Francis Drake begins his circumnavigation of the world in *Pelican*.
'80 – Sir Francis Drake completes his circumnavigation.
– Conversion to Roman Catholicism declared to be treason in England.
Galileo discovers the Law of the Pendulum.
'83 – Plot against the Queen's Life discovered and scotched.
– Humphrey Gilbert takes possession of Newfoundland in the name of the Queen.
'84 – Sir Walter Raleigh discovers Virginia and names it after the Queen. He arranges for its colonization.
'86 – England wins the battle of Zutphen. Sir Philip Sidney dies in this battle.
– Plot against the Queen is discovered. Mary Queen of Scots is implicated in this and is accused of high treason.
– Thomas Cavendish begins the third circumnavigation of the globe.
'87 – Mary Queen of Scots executed for treason.
– Rose Theatre built by Henslowe.
'88 – Sir Francis Drake defeats the Spanish Armada.
'89 – Galileo publishes the results of his experiments with falling bodies.
'92 – John Davis discovers the Falkland Islands.
'93 – Absence from the Church on Sundays made punishable by law.

1595 – Robert Southwell the mystic poet is executed for celebrating Mass.

'96 – England, France and Netherlands form alliance against Spain.

'97 – Beggary made illegal. Statutory provision for Poor Relief shows social responsibility.

– Second Spanish Armada sent against England is destroyed by a storm.

'98 – The Bodleian Library begun. Globe theatre opened.

1601 – Earl of Essex rises in revolt against the Queen and is executed.

'02 – The East India Co. sends its first trading fleet to Sumatra.

'03 – Queen Elizabeth dies. Accession of King James VI of Scotland as James I of England.

'04 – Peace with Spain.

– Banishment of Roman Catholic priest provokes. Gunpowder Plot to blow up Parliament.

– Acts against priests and recusants. Anglican canons made.

– Silk manufacture begun in England.

'05 – Gunpowder Plot discovered. Chief conspirator Guy Fawkes arrested.

– English colonists land in Barbadoes.

'07 – First permanent settlement in Jamestown founded in American mainland.

'08 – Failure of plan for union with Scotland.

– Invention of the microscope and telescope in Netherlands.

'10 – Judicial decision against royal proclamations.

– Explorer Hudson sails through Hudson Bay.

'11 – Parliament dissolved.

– Land granted in North Ireland to Scottish and English Protestants.

'12 – Alliance with German Protestant princes.

– Witches hanged at Lancashire, the last recorded execution for heresy.

1613 – Princes Elizabeth marries Elector Frederick V.
'16 – Shakespeare dies.
– Sir Walter Raleigh sets out in search of El Dorado.

This table shows at a glance how insecure was the throne for Elizabeth when she ascended it. Both at home and abroad she had to maintain a precarious position. In England itself plots against her were being continually hatched though none of them succeeded. Abroad there was continuous warfare with France and Spain. Worst of all was Mary Queen of Scots who was her own cousin. But the Queen dealt with her with a firm hand and she met with the fate a traitor deserves. After this the Queen became comparatively secure and then there set in a time not only of peace and prosperity but of achievements. This was largely because the Queen was a far-sighted stateswoman as well as a patriotic one. This is the most apparent in her attitude to religion. She was liberal in her religious policy. G.M. Trevelyan, a noted social historian, pointed out:

> In the year in which the Queen succeeded her sister Mary, Puritanism was mainly a foreign doctrine imported from Geneva and Rhineland, when she died it was rootedly and characteristically English.[1]

In other words, she helped establish Anglicanism in the country. She passed laws that harmed no one but made religion an essential part of life:

> At the end of her reign, it had become a real religion; its services were dear to many, after more than forty years of use in the ancient churches of England.[2]

Shakespeare's lifetime covered parts of both Queen Elizabeth's and King James's reign, so his adulthood saw equal insecurity at the time of her death. She left no undisputed heir to the throne, so speculation was rife about the succession long before her death, till finally King James of Scotland was brought to England and once more things became settled.

Elizabeth's time was a time of extension and adventure. Society itself encouraged this spirit. Within the social structure class-division was an important feature. But, contrary to modern concepts, these were accepted so that class wars did not impede growth. On one hand, there were the feudal lords and the landed gentry and on the other there were the working classes, but each had his own place and there was freedom for all, opportunities for all. There was no real barrier between the classes:

> English society was based not on equality but freedom—freedom of opportunity and freedom of personal intercourse. Such was the England known and approved by Shakespeare.[3]

It was a society in which dignity of labour was not just a concept but a fact of life. This helped self-reliance and self-respect because each took pride in a work efficiently done and for which he was properly paid.

Social sense of responsibility was there as is apparent in the attitude towards the poor. Beggary was made illegal and at the same time the Poor Law was passed for the relief of the poor. Everyone was also assured of justice by the installing of the system of Justice of Peace. Influential and respectable persons were made JPs to administer justice in minor cases in their own areas. They were controlled by the Privy Council, a country-wide organization.

The economic side of society received great encouragement as the factory system started. This in its turn boosted industrial prosperity for one is dependent on the other. Mining processes improved so that many metals that had been scarce formerly, like lead, copper, iron, and tin became available. Two significant events that improved domestic life took place. Coal became cheaper, so hearth and home became warm and glass became easily available. So window-panes of glass could be afforded by all, so houses became lighter and brighter.

It has already been pointed out that it was a time of exploration and expansion. One of the greatest contributors to the nation's glory was Sir Francis Drake. He completed the circumnavigation of the world and defeated the Spanish Armada. Of these the latter was appreciated the more by common people because it put an end to the threat from the sea and encouraged trade. A second Armada, sent a few years later, perished in a storm. This confirmed and encouraged the belief that the English were the favoured of the gods—meant to succeed. G.M. Trevelyan sums it up:

> By the end of Queen Elizabeth's reign, not only was English commerce and finance thus revising and expanding on a modern basis, but her ancient rivals were in rapid decline.[4]

The Jacobeans not only continued but added to this prosperity and expansion for the age of colonization began. When Shakespeare arrived in London it was only one mile in area but it rapidly expanded later.

During the next forty years, the changes that took place were political changes which did not affect the industrial or agricultural aspect of society. The two royal families of England and Scotland became united when King James VI of Scotland succeeded to the throne of England as King James I. He was a scholarly and a peaceable man and in the first year of his reign he made peace with Spain. So the seas became permanently safe and the great age of colonization started. Settlers from England started going out to and founding colonies in America. This was as yet unrealized beginning of the future British empire. The Virginia Company and the Massachusetts Bay Company came into existence and started organizing emigration. The motives behind the emigration were religious as well as commercial. Again one turns to G.M. Trevelyan for a succinct summing up. He puts Shakespeare against this background just as we are trying to do:

> His works could never have been produced in any other period than those late Elizabethan and early Jacobean times in which it was his luck to live.[5]

(B) THE LITERARY BACKGROUND

A comparison has often been drawn by scholars between the Italian Renaissance and that in England. In Italy, the spirit of the Renaissance expressed itself mainly through painting and sculpture while in England it burst forth in literature. Poetry, drama, prose, novel—every field poured forth a wealth of works unprecedented before and never equalled after. It was in this fertile soil that Shakespeare's works were rooted. A Chronological Table of the main literary events is given below. Some works of the continent have also been mentioned. It is not possible to mention all the works of literature published or written and circulated privately, as often happened at that time. The table begins with the first performance of *Ralph Roister Doister*, ten years before our poet's birth. His works are not mentioned, for that is a matter for later consideration (*vide* Chap. 3 *infra*). Let the student remember that only a fraction of the work produced has been mentioned. The births and deaths of noted literary figures have also been mentioned.

A Chronological Table

1554 – Sir Philip Sidney and Lyly born. *Ralph Roister Doister* performed. Bandello's stories published.

'57 – Tottel's *Miscellany.*

'58 – Kyd, Greene, Peele, Lodge born.

'61 – *Gorboduc* performed. Bacon born. Castiglione's *The Courtier.*

'63 – Drayton and Donne born.

'64 – Shakespeare, Marlowe and Galileo born.

'66 – Gascoigne's *Supposes.* Pointer's *Palace of Pleasure,* Vol. I.

'67 – Campion and Nashe born (team of university wits completed). *Palace of Pleasure*, Vol. II.

'70 – Roger Ascham's (the Queen's tutor) *The Schoolmaster.*

'72 – Camoens (Spain) *Os Lusiados.*

'73 – Tasso's (Italy) *Aminta.*

'75 – Heywood and Tourneur born.

– *Appius and Virginia, Gammer Gurton's Needle,* Fleming's translation of Virgil's *Bucolics* and *Georgics.*

'76 – *The Paradise of Dainty Devises.*

'77 – Holinshed's *Chronicles.*

'78 – Lyly's *Euphues.*

'79 – Spenser's *Shepherd's Calendar*. Lord North's translation of Plutarch's *Lives*. Gosson's *School of Abuse.*

'80 – Montaigne's (France) *Essais* Bks I and II.

'82 – Hakluyt's *Voyages*, Kyd's *Spanish Tragedy.*

1586 – Sir Philip Sidney dies. Lyly's *Endimion.*

'87 – Marlowe's *Tamburlaine*, Lyly's *Gallathea, The Misfortunes of Arthur.*

'89 – Marlowe's *Jew of Malta*. Puttenham's *Arte of English Poesie.*

'90 – *Faerie Queens* Bks. I-III pub. Lodge's *Rosalynde,* Sidney's *Arcadia.*

'91 – Sidney's *Astrophel and Stella*, Peele's *Old Wives' Tale,* Marlowe's *Edward II,* Sir John Harrington's transl. of Ariosto's *Orlando Furioso* at the Queen's order.

'92 – Revised *Arcadia*, Daniel's *To Delia*, Marlowe's *Hero and Leander*, *Arden of Feversham* (Anon.).

'95 – Spenser's *Amoretti* (sonnet-sequence), Sidney's *Apology for Poetry.*

'99 – Spenser dies. Davies's *Nosce Teipsum*, Ben Jonson's *Every Man Out of His Humour.*

1600 – *England's Helicon*, *England's Parnassus*. Ben Jonson's *Cynthia's Revels.*

'01 – Dekker and Marston's *Satiromastix*, Ben Jonson's *Poetaster,* Marston's *What You Will.*

'03 – Dowland's *Third Book of Songs,* Heywoods's *A Woman Killed with Kindness*, Jonson's *Sejanus*, Marston's *The Dutch Courtezan.*

'04 – Chapman's *Bussy D'Ambois,* Marston's *The Malcontent.*

'05 – Drayton's *Collected Poems*, Bacon's *Advancement of Learning*, collaborated play *Eastward Ho!*, Middleton's *A Trick to Catch the Old One.*

'06 – Lyly dies, *Yorkshire Tragedy* (Anon.), Jonson's *Volpone,* Tourneur's *The Revenger's Tragedy.*

'07 – Beaumont and Fletcher's *Knight of the Burning Pestle.*

'08 – Fuller and Milton born. Chapman's *Duke of Byron.*

'09 – Beaumont and Fletcher's *Philaster,* Fulke Greville's *Mustapha*, Tourneur's *The Atheist's Tragedy.*

'10 – Donne's *Pseudo Martyr*, Jonson's *The Alchemist.*

1911 – Spenser's *Collected Works. The Authorised Version of the Bible. A King and no King.*

'12 – Crashaw born. Chapman's *Iliad* I–XXIV. Donne's *Second Anniversarie*, Drayton's *Poly-Olbion*, Webster's *The White Devil.*

'13 – Canstable and Overbury die. *Purchas His Pilgrimage.*

'14 – Overbury's *Characters*. Lodge's *Works of Seneca.*

'15 – Sir Walter Raleigh's *History of the World*. Jonson's *Bartholomew Fair,* Webster's *Duchess of Malfi.*

'16 – Shakespeare dies. Jonson given royal pension. Chapman's *Whole Works of Homer*. Ben Jonson's *The Devil is an Ass.*

As even a brief glance at this table shows, the century from Sir Philip Sidney's birth in 1554 to Shakespeare's death in 1616 may be said to cover the best efflorescence in England. The emblem for the Tudor dynasty was a rose and taking that to stand for English literature, what Sidney saw was only a bud (the staging of *Gorboduc*) compared to the full-blown rose that it eventually came to be. Referring to drama only, Sidney saw it at its birth. It is not surprising that he said:

> Our tragedies and comedies not without cause cried against, observing rules neither of honest civility nor of skilful poetry: excepting *Gorboduc* (again I say of those that I have seen) which notwithstanding as it is full of stately speeches and well-sounding phrases, climbing to the heights of Seneca's style, and as full of notable morality, which it doth most delightfully teach, and so obtains the very end of poesy.[6]

This surprises the modern reader, because *Gorboduc* is of more interest historically today than for anything else. But it was the best tragedy in those days and therefore it is that Sidney praises it. *Ralph Roister Doister* was a comedy and *The Misfortunes of Arthur* was in the nature of a history. All these works are important only according to the first of Arnold's three estimates: the historical. They have no real literary merit.

Turning to other literary forms like narrative poetry, songs and sonnets, the scene is hardly better than that of drama. We are interested in these and not so much in prose and novel because Shakespeare was not interested in the latter. Tottel's famous *Miscellany* containing the sonnets of Wyatt and Surrey had been published but the age of the sonnet-sequence was still in the womb of the future. Spenser's *Shepherd's Calendar* and part of *The Faerie Queene* had been published before Shakespeare's narrative poems. Among these other forms, the one most flourishing was the lyric. The period from 1580-1620 was the golden age of Elizabethan lyrics. This was the time when "the Elizabethan nest of singing-birds" were singing in full-throated ease. The names of the collected songs were inspiring ones also: *The Paradyse of Daynty Devises, England's Parassus, England's Helicon,* etc. Shakespeare took help from these in writing his own songs, mostly light-hearted ones. Even Marlowe, usually a serious writer, wrote one madrigal. Mostly, the songs were light ones:

> The song-lyric, as developed in accordance with the musical art of the time, is too light an instrument to utter the deeper notes of passion and its theme is fanciful love, love that laughs and entreats and sings from very blitheness of soul.[7]

The literary scene prospered as the age advanced. All the genres discussed above grew and branched out into several directions. Prose is of interest to us only as providing sources of Shakespeare's plays but a passing mention should be made of the romances (Sidney's *Arcadia*, Lyly's romances) and philosophical works like those of Bacon, Hooker, Sir Thomas Browne and others. They were all of great importance and influence, especially in the world of thought.

The drama is, for our present purposes, of special interest to us. Kyd's *The Spanish Tragedy* was the first of the plays to be performed by the University Wits (Marlowe, Kyd, Greene, Peele, Nashe). Marlowe's very first attempt *Tamburlaine* became so popular that he quickly wrote a sequel to the play. It came to be taken as a prototype of the conqueror tragedy and came to be emulated, even parodied, in no time. As plays were in great demand theatres were opened by Burbage and Henslowe. The dramatists, thus, could freely experiment with and develop the genre they found to be congenial. Shakespeare's case is different. He did not, like Marlowe, develop only one form, i.e. the conqueror tragedy, but experimented with and perfected different genres. Marlowe was not the only one to settle down with one form. Ben Jonson took up the humour comedy and Beaumont and Fletcher the tragi-comedy. But no one could rival Shakespeare in range or variety or excellence.

The time has come mention the influence of classical writing, specially that of Seneca. It was Kyd who first started it:

> It was the genius of Thomas Kyd that seized upon the essential effect of Senecan action and adopted them, with much relaxation of rules, to the conditions of the public stage. He did this conspicuously in one play, *The Spanish Tragedy*, a strong melodrama in blank verse which became the pattern for many subsequent "revenge" plays.[8]

These rules and the relaxations made of them will be treated in a later chapter (*vide* Chap. 8 *infra*). It is necessary that the student should know a few facts in general. F.T. Bowers, a noted authority, has divided what are called the Blood and Thunder tragedy into four groups: Conqueror Tragedy (Marlowe's tragedies), Revenge Tragedy (*The Spanish Tragedy* is the prototype), Villain Tragedy (*The Changeling*), Domestic Tragedy (*A Woman Killed with Kindness*). Many tragedies cannot be conveniently labeled. Webster's *The Duchess of Malfi* is a revenge tragedy as well as a domestic one. Shakespeare wrote and excelled in all four. His tragedies belong to more than one group. *Othello,* for example, is a domestic tragedy as well as a villain one. *King Lear* transcends all groups *Macbeth* is a conqueror tragedy.

This play, which is to be studied, is a tragedy, but Shakespeare wrote comedies too, so some information about comedy is necessary. Different kinds of comedies flourished in the hands of different writers. M.C. Bradbrook has divided Elizabethan society into three levels and named the contemporary comedies after each. Classified, they stand: The Court, The Country and The City. Shakespeare's comedies come mostly under the first.

Masques were another kind of plays written mostly for the court. Ben Jonson's masques were very well-known ones. Shakespeare uses masques in many of his comedies.

Four centuries after Shakespeare another poet with the benefit of hindsight as well as penetrating analysis points out:

> No poet, no artist of any art, has his complete meaning alone. His significance, his appreciation is the appreciation of his relation to the dead poets and artists.[9]

References

1. G.M. Trevelyan, *Illustrated English Social History*, Vol. 2: Harmondsworth, Penguin Books Ltd., 1964, p. 86.
2. *Ibid.*
3. *Ibid.*, p. 62.
4. *Ibid.* p. 123.
5. *Ibid.*, p. 125.
6. D.J. Enright and Ernst de Chickera (eds.), *English Critical Texts: 16th Century to 20th Century*. Oxford: Oxford University Press, 2002, p. 40.
7. Frederick Ives Carpenter, *English Lyric Poetry: 1500-1700*. London: Blackie and Son Ltd., No date, p. 47.
8. Hardin Craig, *The Literature of the English Renaissance: 1485-1660*. New York: Collier Books, 1862, p. 80.
9. T.S. Eliot, *Three Essays*, Calcutta: Oxford University Press, 1979, p. 17.

2
Life and Works

(A) A SHORT BIOGRAPHY

Usually, details about people of more than four centuries ago are difficult to come by, but a lot is known about Shakespeare's life. The reason is more social than literary. It is true that he gained great literary importance during his own lifetime but so did Marlowe and Ben Jonson and many others. A social historian or a student of economics might cynically say that so many particulars are known about him because his family was rich and influential, but it is also true that he had become a legendary figure even while he lived and many tales have collected around his name, specially about his early days. Later, when his company became accepted by the court, details about his life became well-known and historically true ones. Many biographies of him are available. Among the early ones are Fuller's brief biography in *Worthies* (1662) and John Aubrey's in his *Lives of Eminent Men*. Nicholas Rowe was the first modern author and he took many other sources as well as the biographies available to him. A chronological table of the important events of his life is given below. His works have also been mentioned.

A Chronological Table

1564 – Apr. 23, supposed date of his birth.

– Apr. 26, Shakespeare christened at the local parish church of Stratford-upon-Avon.

'71 – Probably, he is enrolled in the local school.

'78 – The family suffers reverses in fortune because of which he is withdrawn from school this year or perhaps later.

'82 – He gets married to Anne Hathaway.

1583 – Birth of Susanna, his first child.

'85 – The twins, Hamnet and Judith, are born.

'86 – He is supposed to depart for London.

'93 – *Venus and Adonis* pub. by Richard Field, a fellow villager.

'94 – *Rape of Lucrece* pub. *Titus Andronicus* staged, *The Taming of the Shrew.*[1]

'95 – *A Midsummer Night's Dream.*

'96 – Tragic death of Hamnet his only son, at 12 years.

'97 – He buys New Place, the second largest property in his village. *The Merchant of Venice.*

'99 – He buys some shares in the Globe Theatre. *Much Ado About Nothing, As You Like It, Twelfth Night, Henry IV, Julius Caesar.*

1602 – Birth of his first grandchild. He buys one hundred and seven acres of land. *All's Well That Ends Well, Troilus and Cressida, Hamlet.*

'04 – His company taken under royal patronage and given the name of the King's Men. *Measure for Measure, Othello.*

'05 – *Macbeth.*

'06 – *King Lear.*

'07 – *Timon of Athens.*

'09 – *Coriolanus. Sonnets* published.

'11 – He retires from the company and comes back to his native village. *The Winter's Tale, The Tempest.*

'12 – *Henry VIII.*

'16 – His Last Will and Testament drawn up.

– Apr. 23: He dies on his fifty-second birth anniversary.

– Apr. 25: He is buried in the chancel of the Stratford-upon-Avon Church.

The exact date of his birth is not known but the baptism is registered in the parish church in official Latin, so it is known. This used to be often the case. The register says:

1564, Apr. 26: Gulielmus Filius Johannes Shakespeare.[2]

Maybe it was the prevalence of infant mortality because of which babies used to be baptized three days after the birth. This has made scholars assume that he was born on the 23rd. This was the day sacred to St. George, the patron Saint of England. It was a lucky day.

His father did not belong to the class of landed gentry, so he was not regarded as a gentleman, but he was well-respected in society. Shakespeare was the eldest son and the family was prosperous, as his father was in the trade. He later became the alderman of his village which by then had become big enough to have one. By this time he could also claim the status of a gentleman and in view of the feudal structure of society this was very significant. The mother's father belonged to the class of landed gentry—which means that her family was socially of a higher class.

There was the wonderful, peaceful English countryside all around the village and the child Shakespeare would run wild among the greenery. It was the memory of this childhood that made him produce the wonderful description of nature in his poetry (as in *A Midsummer Night's Dream*). But he was not the person to shirk reality. So while the Forest of Arden gives us benevolent nature, he also mentions the freezing skies in his songs.

His father, as has been pointed out, occupied a high position. He was a Justice of Peace (*vide* Chapter 2 *supra*) and the High Bailiff of Stratford. His duties were connected with law courts and Shakespeare often accompanied him there. He gained first-hand knowledge of legal procedures of which the Trial Scene of *The Merchant of Venice* is the result.

Coming now to his schooling, Queen Elizabeth, in order to educate the common people, had established grammar schools all over the country. Shakespeare was admitted to the local grammar school, probably at seven years of age. He was a most reluctant schoolboy. It is thought that when he wrote about "the whining schoolboy"[3] in *As You Like It* he was probably referring to himself.

In these schools, Latin grammar was the most important part of the curriculum. Ben Jonson had ridiculed his "small Latin and less Greek", but this does not mean he did not get any classical education at all. He got what every boy in his time did. All of the schools followed the same hours and the same curriculum. There were definite rules about the daily life. School started at six in the morning, to continue till five in the evening. This might seem to be very long, but there were breaks during the day. There had to be two and half hours' break spaced out throughout the day. The books to be studied were:

Poetry: *The Bucolica of Mantuan*
The Eclogues and the Aeneid of Virgil
The Poems of Horace
The Metamorphoses of Ovid.
Prose: *Caesar, Livy, Cicero.*
Drama: *The Tragedies of Seneca*
The Comedies of Plautus
The Comedies of Terence.

Shakespeare thus had a firm foundation of classical education. He was not a classical scholar according to the standards of the day but he had a good working knowledge. The classical references in his plays come from first-hand knowledge. One of his biographers comments:

> There is no display of learning in any one of plays which could not have been acquired at the Stratford Grammar school.[4]

There is even a story that Shakespeare had taught in a school when young. It is John Aubrey, one of the earliest English biographers, who has given this detail. He had heard an actor say that he:

> ...understood Latin pretty well for he had been in his young days a schoolman in the country.[5]

There is, however, another totally different theory of his schooling given by John Dover Wilson. He expounds the theory that Shakespeare may not have attended any school at all. The family was a Catholic one and there were many Catholic nobles who took in children wanting to live and study. They became part of the family and thus learnt the ways of the nobility and details of their family life at first-hand. It was no easy matter to know the domestic lifestyle of the aristocracy as Shakespeare seems to have known.

After some years misfortune visited the family. It is not known exactly what had happened, but he was taken out of school. He was at the crucial age of learning. At this stage a young boy learns quickly and well. It is not known whether he had completed his education. Neither is it known whether this break in education at this stage was to affect his writing. A.L. Rowse thinks that he was only thirteen then. Referring to the misfortunes of John Shakespeare, he remarks:

> At the time when this blow fell—not a catastrophe but still a blow to pride and status—the alderman's sharp and sensitive son was a boy at the unlucky age of thirteen.[6]

It is important to know that at this time groups of actors used to visit villages on performing trips. They staged the traditional morality plays as well as the new five-act plays written in imitation of classical models, like *Gorboduc.*

It was at this time (in his teens) that our poet fell under the spell of Anne Hathaway. It was in a village a little distant from his own, named Shottery. Anne Hathaway was the belle of the district. She was an extremely attractive woman, eight years older than him. It has been said, by an unknown admirer in a couplet often quoted by his biographers:

> Anne Hathaway, she hath a way
> To charm all hearts, Anne Hathaway.

She could pick and choose among her admirers and it was Shakespeare she chose and agreed to marry. The age barrier did not matter to the lovers and they got married on Nov. 28, 1582—he not yet nineteen and she twenty-six. Their first child Susanna was born next year, baptised on May 26, 1583. Two years later the twins, Hamnet and Judith, were born. Hamnet was to die in 1596, leaving no one to carry on the line, at the age of twelve.

So Shakespeare was now a young man of barely twenty-one, with three children and a wife to support and no visible source of income. Many legends are there about this time of his life. Told by John Aubrey, one of them tells how he taught in a school. There is another story, a much better-known one. This has been told by the actor Thomas Betterton to Nicholas Rowe and also by a contemporary clergyman. This story is commonly accepted as being true. It is said that our poet, along with some other young men stole a deer from the park of Sir Thomas Lucy at Charlecote. They were all arrested and Sir Thomas ordered them to be whipped and put into prison. How much of this is true is debatable for there were no deer parks in that place at that time. On the other hand, it is definitely true that the forest nearby had many deers and Sir Thomas Lucy had the responsibility of taking care of the game of Warwick. So there may well be some truth in the legend. It is said that Shakespeare resented bitterly the treatment meted out to him and took his revenge on Sir Thomas Lucy by depicting him as the stupid Justice Shallow in *The Merry Wives of Windsor* and *Henry IV*. Again modern researches say that Sir Thomas was not in charge of Charlecote forest at the time. Anyway, it is said that this humiliation was the deciding factor behind his decision to leave for London in 1586.

There is another story that Shakespeare had joined as an actor in one of the companies that toured England, providing entertainment. This idea is based on a certain will in which a different variation of his name has been used. A gentleman of Lancashire had made this will and mentioned William Shakeshafte as a player in his service. On the basis of this, it has been said that:

> ...since Shakeshafte is a variant form of Shakespeare, which the dramatist's own grandfather is known to have used, it has been conjectured that William Shakespeare before his marriage had already served as an actor in the service of a Lancashire gentleman.[7]

This, again, is quite a possible thing for at that time many touring companies travelled the roads. Not only the Queen's Men but other troupes also visited Stratford. For example in 1583 alone there were three well-known groups which played there: the Earl of Worcester's Men, the Earl of Oxford's Men and the Earl of Essex's Men. In 1586, another company was there whose name is not known. Again, in 1587, which is probably the year in which he left for London, the Earl of Essex's Men and the Earl of Leicester's Men had also visited the place. Biographers think that he had not only watched the plays but had also acted in them. Hamlet's conversation with the players give evidence of intensive first-hand knowledge of stagecraft. Perhaps he had also been accepted as one of the actors in one of these itenerant companies and gone to London with them.

The period from 1586 to 1592 is known as the Dark Years as very little is known about them. Anecdotes are many, since nothing can be really proved. One legend says that he had tended to the horses of the gentlemen who came to watch the plays and thus earned a pittance. It is also said that he was assistant to a promoter. But this much is known for sure: that he found a fellow villager, Richard Field, who had left the village before him and was now an established printer. In 1593, this friend published his *Venus and Adonis* and *The Rape of Lucrece* next year. Both of these became very popular. His literary career can be said to have begun with narrative poems.

Marlowe was his only serious rival at the time. As can be seen in the chronological table given above the two had been born at the same time and had reached London at the same time. This decade of the eighties was a particularly inspiring one. Sir Francis Drake was ravaging the Spanish Main and Sir Philip Sidney was writing the first sequence of love-sonnets *Astrophel and Stella* and was most probably drafting his monumental prose romance *Arcadia*. Spenser, out there in Ireland, was writing his poetical monument *The Faerie Queene*. The University Wits were converging towards London. Lyly, who was the leader of the group had already produced *Euphues* and was turning towards drama. Two of his romantic comedies had been performed by choir of the Chapel Royal for the Queen in 1584. But of all his works it was *Euphues* that brought him lasting fame. It became very popular with the ladies, so much so that Lyly had said that:

> *Euphues* had rather lie shut in a lady's
> casket than open on a scholar's study.[8]

London was already the centre of cultural and other activities. The University Wits were firmly established and new horizons were opening everywhere. This was the London to which Shakespeare came, buzzing with activity, flowing with the glory of achievement. F.E. Halliday remarks of this that:

> Shakespeare had arrived at London at the most thrilling moment in its history; thrilling, however, not only because of danger, anxious expectations and hope in the air, but also because the long-awaited dramatic revival was now imminent.[9]

Shakespeare must have been soaking up knowledge and impressions and had been firmly consolidating his position against this background. This was all the more so because his literary works had become important enough to attract the envious and rather contemptuous notice of Greene, one of the University Wits. He was the first contemporary to have mentioned his name. It occurs in a pamphlet which, ironically enough, is remembered today only because of this reason. It is named "Greene's Groats-worth of Wit Bought with a Million of Repentance". It contains a letter at the end addressed to the others of his group, Peele, Nashe, and Marlowe. In it he warns them against actors, specially against a certain actor in an allusive manner, leaving one in no doubt as to who it is he is referring to:

> Yes, trust them not: for there is an upstart crow, beautified with our feathers that with his Tyger's heart wrapt in a Player's hyde, supposes he is as well able to bombast out a blank verse as the best of you: and being an absolute Johannes Factotum is in his own conceit the only Shake-scene in a country.[10]

There are two clear hints here about the identity of our poet. The line "Tyger's heart wrapt in a Player's hyde" is a deliberately misquoted line from his *Henry VI,* Pt. III: "O tiger's heart wrapped in a woman's hide". Then there is the satirical allusion to "shake-scene" which of course refers to our poet. This is spiteful and jealous, but it also proves that he had become alarming enough to cause envy in an established writer. This reference was in 1592 and from now on there are occasional bits of reference to him. To the sophisticated and highly educated University Wits he must have appeared as an uneducated yokel from the country. To have achieved this in six years, against bitter competition and totally alien environment is no mean feat.

These are the years known as the years of apprenticeship. But it was not that he was merely learning, for he was producing as well. The two narrative poems, the sonnet-sequence to Mr. W.H., the *Henry VI* trilogy, *Richard III*, *Titus Andronicus*, *The Comedy of Errors, Love's Labour's Lost*, *The Two Gentlemen of Verona*, and *The Taming of the Shrew* were all produced at this time and were all highly successful. A coarse tragedy like the blood-and-thunder *Titus Andronicus* was so popular that it was published in 1594, with the title-page revealing its success:

> ...as it was played by the Right Hon. the Earl of Derby, the Earl of Pembroke, and the Earl of Sussex their servants.[11]

All of these were well-known companies and it also becomes clear that the play had been performed in quick succession. It seems surprising that a play like this had been so popular, for it is the most unsubtle, the coarsest of his plays. But the Elizabethans loved it.

The list of the works given above is very suggestive. As has been pointed out before (*vide* Introduction, *supra*), he didn't confine himself to one genre. So there is the courtly romance of *Love's Labour's Lost* (which according to modern critics was the very first play he wrote), as well as tragedies and histories. Then there are the sonnets and the narrative poems. No other dramatist was so versatile. Shakespeare had proved himself a master, in every field, and this was only a beginning. The best was still to come. Indeed, Greene had ample cause to be alarmed, though he did not know the half of it.

He had joined the group of Lord Chamberlaine's Men by this time and was an important member of it. The receipt of plays produced at Court by the Royal Treasury contains the names of our poet, Kempe and Burbage. He continued with this company till the very end. It presaged a fruitful period because each needed the other. The company needed a writer in order to be continually productive and a writer needed a company to produce his plays. A happy symbiosys. Plays of course were popular and a company had to be productive in order to survive.

It was probably at this time that he paid a visit to his village. His father was in his sixties, a venerable paterfamilias of a large family of many children and grandchildren. His own children too were growing up. Susanna was nine and the twins were seven years old Shakespeare stayed here for four months and probably wrote *Richard III* and *Venus and Adonis* at this time. The poem is dedicated to the Earl of Southampton, "the onlie begetter" of his famous sonnet-sequence. It is time now to talk about this legendary friendship between the two.

The Earl was a well-known patron of the arts and Shakespeare was very fortunate in getting his patronage. It is said that the Earl's mother had despaired of getting him to marry and asked Shakespeare to write something to persuade him to do so. The first ten sonnets of the sequence, known as "the procreation sonnets" were the result. Thereafter developed a long and intense relationship between the two. The sonnets tell the story of this relationship. Then after some time a Dark Lady whom the poet loved was introduced to the Earl. The two fell in love. This is the harrowing story told by the sonnets—a story of betrayed friendship and betrayed love. The Earl is not named anywhere. In the dedication he is called Mr. W.H. and it is thought that this refers to Henry Wriothesley, the Earl of Southampton, an extremely handsome young nobleman.

The sonnets display Petrarchan love at its most intense and the dedication to *The Rape of Lucrece* rings with the intensity of this love:

> The love I dedicate to your Lordship is without end...what I have done is yours, and what I have to do is yours, being part in all I have devoted yours.[12]

An artist without any regular and certain source of income needed a patron in those days and our poet had that in this Earl. He was so prosperous that he was able to buy a share in his own company whereas Greene was languishing in poverty and sickness. A.L. Rowse has pointed out:

> It meant all the difference between the dreadful insecurity poor Greene had, and others, died of, and having firm ground under his feet.[13]

How very lucky Shakespeare was in everything can be made out if we take a look at the background. First of all, his company, apart from public performances, gave thirty-two stagings in the Queen's court—an almost unique distinction for any theatrical company. He was the only playwright to survive the Plague. Kyd was already dead at the age of thirty-two and Marlowe was suddenly killed at a drunken brawl—as is well known. The other members of the University Wits were almost at the end of their productivity. Ben Jonson was the only dramatist of a like calibre, but he had not yet come, and when he was to come he was to busy himself with satirical comedy, almost the only genre untouched by Shakespeare. His star was high indeed in the sky.

It was time for the early comedies. He was a successful man-about-town and this is reflected in his plays Lord Berowne of *Love's Labour's Lost* is supposed to be a portrait of himself. He was the gayest and the wittiest of the Lords in this play. In 1594, our poet was twenty-nine, in the full flower of his creative energy. An Oxford undergraduate named Henry Willoughby mentions his name in a poem.

> Yet Tarquin plucked his glistering grape
> And Shakespeare paints poor Lucrece's rape.[14]

This worshipful young man presents Shakespeare as a worldly-wise man-about-town who gives advice about one's love affairs.

While he was writing *King John* in 1597, he had the harrowing experienced of losing his only son and heir Hamnet. No one was left to carry on the line. Anoher significant fact, a happy one, that happened at this time concerns his entire family. There is always an upward movement in society. Men of lower rank try to ascend higher in the scale. So Shakespeare's father had been trying to climb up into the lower ranks of nobility by getting a coat-of-arms and had applied at the Herald's College for one, but without success. Now, like a dutiful son, our poet tried to fulfill his father's wishes by pursuing the matter. This time the request was granted. This gave his family the status of landed gentry, a matter of great importance in a feudal society. He also bought New Place which was the second best house in the village, the first being the Town Hall. Stratford had grown into a small town. This, more than anything else, gives one an idea of his social status.

By the next year (1598), he was so much of an accepted master dramatist that in *Palladis Tamia* Francis Meres gives an account of him thus:

> ...the sweet wittie soule of Ovid lives in mellifluous and hony-tonged Shakespeare, witness his *venus and Adonis*, his *Lucrece*, his sugred sonnets among his friends.[15]

Besides mentioning these, Meres gives a list of his plays staged till them, which has been of great help to scholars in determining the dates of his plays. Meres, like Ben Jonson, worshipped the man "this side idolatry" since he asserted that Shakespeare was the contemporary equivalent of Terence and Plautus in comedy and of Seneca in tragedy.

Meanwhile the Queen passed away in 1603 and King James VI of Scotland acceded to the throne of England as King James I. Shakespeare's company came under his own patronage under the name of the King's Men. The men of the company would have the royal livery to wear and take part in all the royal pageants and processions, the highest honour any group can have. From this point onwards many facts about our poet become available. There are legal documents proving how he went on changing his dwelling place from Bishopgate to Southwark to Cripple-gate. He bought a house at Blackfriar in 1613 and never occupied it. In 1602, he bought a hundred and seven acres of land for farming and later bought a cottage and a quarter acre of land. He continued writing for and acting in his company. A document shows that he had acted in Ben Jonson's historical tragedy *Sejanus*.

It was in 1603 that, after producing another play in London, he started producing his Four Great Tragedies. *Hamlet* was performed in 1602. This was his last play in the Elizabethan Age. *Othello* the first of his Jacobean plays was staged in 1604 and performed at Court. It is a well-known fact that in general there is a difference between the Elizabethan and the Jacobean ages in spirit and this change is reflected in his plays. The Elizabethan exuberance and optimism was succeeded in the Jacobean age by doubt and conflict. Theodore Spencer has remarked:

> The earlier Renaissance had emphasized man's potentialities by comparing man with the angels, the later Renaissance emphasized their destruction by comparing man with animals.[16]

Shakespeare's plays too reflect this sombre attitude. All the tragedies (except *Hamlet*) and the problem plays belong to the Jacobean period. They all concern themselves with the problem of evil as indeed is the case with the play under discussion. But as the years passed these troubled waters were left behind and he emerged into the calm sea of the last romances. His sonnet-sequence was published in 1609 and in 1611 (according to Irving Ribner) he retired to Stratford. In the meantime his mother had passed away and the first grandchild was born, both signifying the coming of old age.

Though he retired from active life, on the stage his concerns with London did not cease. This, besides other facts is best proved by the performance of *The Tempest* to celebrate a royal betrothal in which he himself enacted the role of Prospero to bless the royal couple.

Now the last stage of his life was drawing near. In 1616, his will was drawn up and two months later, on 23rd April which was his birthday he passed away at fifty-four years of age. His will is to be seen in Somerset House.

There are many rich and complex symbols adorning his grave. A bust of him is there with a quill in his hand to signify that he was a writer. Allegorical figures of Rest and Labour stand at the sides beside columns. His coat-of-arms is of course there and a skull on top, to signify that Death conquers all. There is a Latin couplet and a sextet in English. There is also an epitaph which is thought to have been written by the poet himself but some scholars think it to be too crude for him. It might have been written by an official epitaph-writer.

These are the words and it is difficult to think that Shakespeare had written them:

Good friend, for Jesus sake forbeare
To dig the dust enclosed here!
Blest be the man that spares these stones
And curst be he that moves my bones.[17]

References

1. The dates for these works have been taken from *The New Caxton Encyclopaedia*. London, Caxton Pubs. Ltd.
2. Cited in F.E. Halliday, *The Life of Shakespeare*. London, Gerald Duckworth Co. Ltd., 1961, p. 20.
3. *As You Like It*, Act III, sc. vii, ll. 145-47, p. 38. Wordsworth Classics, 1993.
4. Irving Ribner, *William Shakespeare: Life, Times and Theatre*. London, John Wiley and Sons Inc. '69, pp. 38-39.
5. Quoted in Rowse, *William Shakespeare: A Biography*. London, Macmillan & Co. Ltd., 1963, p. 58.
6. Rowse, *op. cit.*, p. 34.
7. Ribner, *op. cit.*, p. 44.
8. Hardin Craig, *The Literature of the English Renaissance: 1485-1660*. New York, Collier Books, 1862, p. 52, citation.
9. F.E. Halliday, *op. cit.* p. 60.
10. Quoted in I. Ribner, *op. cit.*, p. 45.
11. Quoted in A.L. Rowse, *op. cit.*, p. 201.
12. Quoted in Halliday, *op. cit.*, pp. 102-03.
13. A.L. Rowse, *op. cit.*, p. 201.
14. Halliday, *op. cit.*, p. 118.
15. *Ibid.*, p. 138 and many others.
16. Theodore Spencer, *Shakespeare and the Nature of Man*. New York, Macmillan & Co., 1945, p. 49.
17. Quoted in Ribner, *op. cit.* p. 64 and many others.

(B) SHAKESPEARE'S WORKS

Scholars, with the help of many contemporary documents have drawn up a chronological scheme of Shakespeare's works. The documents that have been used are works like Henslowe's Diary, the Stationer's Register and others. These give the dates of stage performances not of composition or publication. The dates of performances of many plays are not known and some of the plays, like *Titus Andronicus* were published quite early and some much later. In spite of these difficulties a scheme has been tentatively agreed upon. The different stages into which his career has been divided are however highly flexible and overlap with each other:

Phase I

1591 – *The Comedy of Errors.*

'92 – *The Two Gentlemen of Verona, Henry VI,* Pts. I, II and III.

'93 – *King Richard III, Romeo and Juliet, Venus and Adonis.*

Phase II

1594 – *The Rape of Lucrece, The Sonnets, Titus Andronicus, Richard II, A Midsummer Night's Dream, Love's Labour's Lost, The Taming of the Shrew.*

'95 – *The Merchant of Venice.*

'97 – *Henry IV,* Pt. I.

'98 – *Henry IV,* Pt. II, *The Merry Wives of Windsor.*

'99 – *Henry V, Much Ado About Nothing, Julius Caesar.*

1600 – *As You Like It, Twelfth Night.*

Phase III

1602 – *Hamlet, Troilus and Cressida, All's Well that Ends Well.*

'04 – *Measure for Measure, Othello.*

'05 – *King Lear.*

'06 – *Macbeth.*

'07 – *Antony and Cleopatra.*

'08 – *Coriolanus, Timon of Athens, Pericles.*

Phase IV

1610 – *Cymbeline, The Winter's Tale, The Tempest.*

'11 – *Henry VIII.*

This shows that Shakespeare's career has been divided into four phases which are not mutually exclusive. Some critics think that all the works till *Love's Labour's Lost* are in Phase I. Some on the other hand think that *Pericles* belongs to the Phase IV. Latest research shows that it is *Love's Labour's Lost* which is his first play and not *Comedy of Errors.*

Phase I is known as the Phase of Experiments or Apprenticeship. He was learning his craft at this time, revising or re-writing old plays. As far as versification goes, he made use of couplets and end-stopped lines at this time, which stopped occurring later as he mastered the technique of blank verse. *Love's Labour's Lost* shows play with words. His art of characterization is not well-developed, though he finds a symmetry by balancing one character against another, best seen in *Comedy of Errors.*

1594-95-1601 is the period of development. The Golden Comedies were produced at this time and the chronicle plays too. Blank verse had been mastered and as far as characterization goes he has started to plumb the depths of the human mind. Plots are now more neatly made. He has become a better dramatist, everything considered.

Phase III shows further development, but in a different direction. Shakespeare has mastered his craft by this time. It is the change in his attitude towards the world and men that is remarkable at this time. No longer are there any light-hearted characters. In fact, light-heartedness has itself disappeared. He looks at the world with a firm eye and does not find it pleasing. Henri Fluchère has remarked of this period:

> The conflict between good and evil, ugliness and beauty, innocence and crime, purity and impurity, hope and disgust, love and hate, order and disorder natural laws and the anarchy produced by the passions—all was resolved in Shakespeare's so-called "dark period" with an infinite despair.[1]

The Last Phase or the Romance period lasts from 1608 to 1612. During this time, the last four Romances were written. Shakespeare has now achieved the serenity, the wisdom that comes from age. He calmly accepts the presence of evil as inevitable and looks forward to the future that a new generation will create a better world. Fluchère says:

> As his career drew to a close Shakespeare turned back to his youth and his implicit theme is always that of fertility, resurrection, joy of life.[2]

There has always been controversy about the authorship of *King Henry VIII*. Scholars have argued in ascribing it to him. *The Two Noble Kinsmen*, it is agreed, was a work of collaboration with Fletcher. In the brief account of his works given below it has been tried to keep a more or less chronological order as far as possible. This has not been easy as the dates of performance and that of composition, differ with different documents, it is not possible to be exact. *Macbeth* falls between *King Lear* and *Antony and Cleopatra*, but, as the present book itself is devoted to this work, it has not been mentioned. *The Two Noble Kinsmen* has not been mentioned either.

BRIEF NOTES ON HIS WORKS

The Comedy of Errors

This play, staged in 1594, is his shortest one. Many scholars think it to be his first. The plot is taken from a comedy of Plautus, *The Menaechmuses*. Plautus has a pair of twins, but Shakespeare has doubled it, making the plot more complex. The characters are neatly balanced against each other. His versification however is at an early stage. In the passage given below for example, there is rhyming, and end-stopped lines till it cannot be called blank verse at all:

> And may it be that you have quite forgot
> A husband's office? Shall, Antipholus
> Even in the spring of love, thy love-springs rot
> Shall love, in building, grow so ruinous?[3]

The Two Gentlemen of Verona

This the first of his romantic comedies, has two pairs of lovers, two servants, and two fathers. The characters are balanced against each other, making a symmetrical pattern. Conflict between love and friendship is the theme, with the emphasis on friendship. The theme of forgiveness and reconciliation, a recurrent one in the last romances, is also there. Crossed love, disguised heroines, exile, etc. appear, as they do in the mature comedies. Julia anticipates Rosalind and Portia, as Silvia does Juliet. By this time his blank verse has improved so much that he has started to use stichomythia in which a line is split up among two or more speakers. This gives the line flexibility plus dramatic quality:

Duke: Which of you saw Sir Eglamour of late?
Thurio: Not I.
Proteus: Nor I
Duke: Saw you my daughter?
Proteus: Neither[4]

Henry VI Pts I, II and III

These chronicle plays brought him much fame. There are ten such plays, including *Henry VIII*. They do not merely record events. The serious themes of the duties and privileges of royalty are also treated. The plays contain much pomp and pageantry, loved by the Elizabethans. The trilogy was staged in 1592 and became so popular that it was staged thrice in eight days. Greene had obliquely referred to one of the lines. It presents a world of ferocity and treason. By now his verse has gained all the sonority and flexibility of a master:

The Queen with all the northern earls and lords
Intends here to besiege you in your castle.
She is hard by with twenty thousand men,
And therefore fortify your hold, my lord.[5]

Richard III

The *Henry VI* trilogy shows the influence of Marlowe in its poetry. In *Richard III,* this influence can be seen in the character of Richard III as well. He is a Marlovian figure and the play, like one of Marlowe, is more of a tragedy than a history. The second longest play of Shakespeare, it is very effective on the stage. It has often been put in a sequence with the preceding trilogy and the whole called a tetralogy. As in a tragedy the figure of the hero dominates the play, evoking pity and terror.

Romeo and Juliet

His most popular romantic tragedy, this tells the story of star-crossed lovers. The hero and the heroine have become the symbol of tragic love. Fate, more than character, takes a hand in the play, as is the case with Greek tragedies. Here family feud takes the place of fate. Character has not, as yet, taken the place of destiny. That is to come later. Some of the speeches and scenes in it have become classics, particularly the Balcony Scene between the lovers and Mercutio's whimsical Queen Mab speech:

> Her waggon-spokes made of long spinners' legs;
> The cover, of the wings of grasshoppers;
> The traces of the smallest spider's web,
> The collars, of the moonshine's watery beams;[6]

Venus and Adonis

Many narrative poems based on classical stories were written at that time and the ones by our poet were very popular. The story is from Ovid and the poem became so popular as to run through ten or eleven editions. It has been written in six-line stanzas or quatrains followed by couplets. It is a neater form than the comparatively unwieldy Spenserian stanza of nine lines made famous by him in the *Faerie Queene*. The stanza of the poem runs thus:

> Even as the sun with purple-coloured face
> Had ta'en his last leave of the weeping main,
> Rose-cheek'd Adonis, hied him to the chase,
> Hunting he lov'd, but love he laugh'd to scorn
> Sick-thoughted Venus makes amain unto him
> And like a bold-fac'd suitor 'gins to woo him.[7]

Rape of Lucrece

This narrative poem, like the preceding one, is also based on Ovid and is dedicated to the Earl of Southampton. It is a more serious poem than the former one for the poet tries to analyse Tarquin's guilt-complex. This attempt raises it above the other light-hearted poems prevalent at that time. Tarquin's psychological conflicts raise him to almost tragic heights. The stanza pattern used is the complex seven-line form of the rhyme royal: ab ab bcc. The famous poem "They Flee from Me" is written in this stanza-pattern.

The Sonnets

There are a hundred and fifty-four sonnets in this famous sequence. It has been already mentioned (*vide* his Life, *supra*) they are thought to be autobiographical and relate the three-cornered relationship between him, Mr. W.H. and the Dark Lady, with the first one getting prominence. The first 126 sonnets depict the intense friendship between him and his patron, Mr. W.H. "the onlie begetter" of the sonnets. The remaining are about him and the Dark Lady who was possibly a maid of honour at Court, Mary Fitton. The sonnets contain immortal lines that immortalize Mr. W.H.'s beauty as well as his own poetry:

> So long as men can breathe or eyes can see
> So long lives this, and this gives life to thee.[8]

Titus Andronicus

This is a true blood-and-thunder tragedy in the Senecan tradition. It is a Roman tragedy and the theme is revenge. It was an extremely popular play at the time, but a most coarse one for moderns.

Richard II

Shakespeare's plays usually do not have topical relevance as this one has. It reflects the contemporary political situation most faithfully, so that the Queen had said, "I am Richard II, know ye that? This tragedy is played forty times in open streets and houses." The play shows the deposition of Richard II and the scene had to be omitted when the play was staged. The King's abdication speech is famous:

> Of comfort no man speak
>
> ....
>
> For God's sake, let us sit upon the ground
> And tell sad stories of the death of kings:
> How some have been depos'd some slain in war,
> Some haunted by the ghosts they have depos'd.[9]

A Midsummer Night's Dream

This is the best of his early comedies. For the first time Shakespeare introduces the supernatural element in it, in the persons of the fairy King and Queen and their attendants. Consequently, the range of characters is a large one. There is wonderful nature poetry and many songs here. The fairies sing a lullaby for Titania:

> You spotted snakes with double tongues
>   Thorny hedgehogs be not seen;
> Newts and blind-worms, do no wrong;
>   Come not near our Fairy Queen.

Oberon gives an enchanting description of nature:

> I know a bank wheron the wild thyme blows
> Where oxlips and the nodding violet grows
> Quite over-capopied with luscious woodbine
> With sweet musk-roses and with eglantine.[10]

It also contains one of his best characters: Bottom.

Love's Labour's Lost

Modern researches show this to have been the very first play of the poet. It is noted for its witty dialogues and witty characters. The characters are from the very highest level: The King and his Lords on the one hand, and the Princess and her Ladies on the other. A passage by Lord Berowne who is supposed to be half autobiographical, renouncing flowery diction, has become famous:

> Taffeta phrases, silken terms precise,
> Three-pil'd hyperboles, spruce affectations
> Figures pedantical; these summer flies
> Have blown me full of maggot ostentation
> I do forswear them.[11]

King John

On the face of it, this play is about King John, but it has contemporary relevance too. Like Queen Elizabeth, King John too had waged a life-long battle with the Church of Rome.

Controversial themes like religion had always been avoided by the poet and this too is not a religious play. It is a highly patriotic one and foreign policy is the most important theme. Shakespeare handles this tricky issue most capably and the character of King John has been depicted with great insight. The parallel with Queen Elizabeth that finally led to her excommunication made it popular.

The Taming of the Shrew

Staged in 1594, the play has an Italian setting. The main theme is that of husband-and-wife relationship, a highly popular one. A very entertaining play, it brings to the fore the poet's ability for creating convincing characters. This is the most evident in the female character he has created as foil for the shrew, thus balancing them neatly.

The Merchant of Venice

This is the first of the Golden Comedies. There is an anomaly in that it is the merchant of the title who should be the hero but it is debatable whether in this play that is the case. Shylock, the villain, is such a strong character that he towers over everybody else. The Elizabethan convention of disguise is used to great effect, for the female characters each, for however short a time, put on male disguises. This play gives unparalleled prose as well:

> Hath not a Jew eyes? hath not a Jew hands organs, dimensions, senses, affections, passions?... If you prick us, do we not bleed? If you tickle us, do we not laugh? if you poison us, do we not die? and if you wrong us, shall we not revenge?[12]

Henry IV Pts I and II

These two plays can hardly be bettered as chronicle plays. One of the reasons is Sir John Falstaff who is the very archetype of comic characters. He is Prince Henry's close companion, but towards the end of the play is rejected by him. He, however, has become immortal: an unparalleled figure:

> A good portly man, i'faith and a corpulent; of a cheerful look, a pleasing eye, and a most notable carriage...there is virtue in that Falstaff: him keep with, the rest banish.[13]

The Merry Wives of Windsor

It is said that Queen Elizabeth was enchanted by Falstaff and wanted to see "the fat knight in love" and so this play was written. This farce begins where *Henry IV* Pt. II ends. It is a rollicking farce, highly stage-worthy. There is, however, points worthy of note in the play. One of them is the fact that Shakespeare has poked fun at Ben Jonson's humour characters. Corporal Nym is such a character and uses the word "humour" in every sentence he speaks. He is, of course, a parody.

King Henry V

It is said that Henry V is Shakespeare's idea of the ideal king. The play has two themes: Kingship and patriotism. The most remarkable feature of the play is the attitude of the poet to the battle of Agincourt. He has shown the positive as well as the negative side of war-bravery as well as suffering. Falstaff "a-babbling of green fields" goes to Arthur's bosom in this play.

Much Ado About Nothing

Of his group of four Golden Comedies, this is the second. The theme of love is presented in two different ways. There is the crude sensual love that ultimately is deceptive, presented in the Hero-and-Claudio plot. Benedick-and-Beatrice plot takes up the rejection of married love. But ultimately the couples come to accept the social responsibilities of love and marriage, though they are unaware of this.

Julius Caesar

This play is a Roman tragedy—a trilogy of which the other two are *Coriolanus* and *Antony and Cleopatra*. The contradistinction between tyranny and liberty is the central theme. The characters are all historical ones, but Shakespeare makes them living human beings as well. He took the story from Plutarch and has adapted many of his passages most artistically. There are many famous speeches in this play. The Forum Speech of Antony is specially famous:

> I come to bury Caesar, not to praise him.
> The evil that men do lives after them,

The good is often interred with their bones;
So let it be with Caesar.[14]

This speech is specially well-known for its use of irony in its description of Brutus.

As You Like It

This play is accepted as the best of the Golden Comedies. It is also called a pastoral comedy as the major part of it takes place in the benevolent lap of nature in the forest of Arden. The one central theme of love is presented in four different ways through four pairs of lovers. The range of characters is considerable since royal and courtly characters are involved as well as humble shepherds. Every Jack has his Jill in the end, with no less than four weddings. Rosalind is easily the most coveted role for any actress, the more so as she nearly spends the whole play in the disguise of a boy. Again this shows how Shakespeare makes fine use of a popular convention when it suits him. The play has some of the most famous songs in Shakespeare. The song by Amiens is specially famous:

Under the greenwood tree
Who loves to lie with me
And turn his merry note
Undo the sweet bird's throat
Come hither, come hither, come hither.[15]

Twelfth Night

This is the fourth and the last of the Golden Comedies. Nearly, all the popular stage conventions are present in disguises, mistaken identities, the separation and re-union of siblings, etc. In addition the separated siblings are identical twins. A somewhat less effective brother of Falstaff is to be found in Sir Toby Belch. Feste is one of the most effective jesters in Shakespeare, rivalled only by that unique character, the Fool in *Lear*. Viola is one of his finest heroines. The Clown sings one of the best songs in his plays:

When that I was a little tiny boy
With hey, ho, and the wind and the rain

A little thing was but a toy
For the rain it doth raineth every day.[16]

Hamlet

This is the last of his Elizabethan plays and the first of the Four Great Tragedies. It ushers in a mood of darkness and conflict which was not to be overcome easily. It is, after all, a revenge tragedy but this feature has receded into the background because, primarily, of the extraordinary importance that the character of Hamlet has gained. His soliloquies are of supreme importance. Most important is the fact how the poet has taken something as crude as the blood-and-thunder revenge tragedy and has subtilised it beyond recognition.

Troilus and Cressida

This play goes back to Ancient Greece for its source. It is the first of his Problem Comedies. This play in particular comes very near to a satire, but not like the satiric comedies. Like all the plays of this group, this also deals with the repulsive, seamy side of life. The "degree speech" delivered by Ulysses is famous:

The heavens themselves, the planets and the centre
Observe degree, priority and place...
...O, when degree is shak'd
Which is the ladder to all high designs
The enterprise is sick.[17]

All's Well That Ends Well

This is the second of the Problem Comedies. It deals with the theme of conflict between virtue and nobility. The Bertram-Helena plot shows this the best but there are many sub-themes like those arising out of generation gaps. Shakespeare's attitude towards follies and vices is far less tolerant than it was formerly as can be seen in the difference between the braggart Parolles and Falstaff.

Measure for Measure

This is another Problem Comedy. Like *As You Like It*, the summiest of the comedies, it ends with four marriages, the only other comedy to do so. It has two themes: Justice and Fidelity.

It contains one of the most enchanting of his songs: "Take O take those lips away."

Othello

Othello is the first of his Jacobean plays and the second of the Four Great Tragedies (*Hamlet* was the first). It is called a later *Romeo and Juliet* as it like the former, treats the theme of jealousy. Iago is one of the most famous villains about whom Coleridge has used one of his most oft-quoted phrases, "motiveless malignity". The play contains some of the best poetic passage in Shakespeare.

King Lear

Present-day scholars agree in regarding this as the best play of Shakespeare. Basically, it treats the theme of the predicaments of man in a cruel universe. Among other things it has been called a cosmic drama. An almost primitive legend has become a terrible tragedy that is nothing short of sublime. The Fool in this play is a unique character, serving many complex purposes. It has often been compared with *The Divine Comedy* of Dante. It contains one of the most effective passages which is also noted for its simplicity:

> Why should a dog, a horse, a rat have life
> And thou no breath at all? Thou'lt come no more
> Never, never, never, never, never.[18]

Antony and Cleopatra

Along with *Julius Caesar* and *Coriolanus,* this play forms the trilogy of Roman Tragedies. The theme of love is predominant. The character of Cleopatra dominates the play from the beginning to the end. It is a very complex play and has been called a history, a symphony, a political play as well as a Roman tragedy. It contains some of his best poetic passages, specially the description of Cleopatra by Enobarbas.

Coriolanus

This is the last of his tragedies and a political Roman tragedy. The hero Coriolanus is a noble that he cannot stoop to any device for cheap popularity. Society rejects him and therein lies his tragedy.

Timon of Athens

This is a five-act Problem Comedy, but Una Ellis-Fermor argues that it is not a complete play. The hero is a misanthrope and rejects society. It leaves us with a sense of incompleteness.

Pericles, Cymbeline, The Winter's Tale, The Tempest

These four plays are known as the Last Romances and treat the same theme of sin, repentance and forgiveness. A tainted, sinful older generation hands the future over to a purer younger generation with the hope that the future may be better. *The Tempest*, the last play was staged to celebrate a royal betrothal. Shakespeare himself enacted the role of Prospero and blessed the royal couple. It is supposed to contain his farewell to the theatre as declared by Prospero in his remunciation speech. Miranda is the prototype of all pure and innocent young girls.

References

1. Fluchère, H., *Shakespeare*. London, Longman and Green, 1953, p. 54.
2. *Ibid*, p. 265.
3. *The Comedy of Errors*, III: ii: 1-4, Craig, W.J. ed. *The Complete Works of William Shakespeare*, London, O.U.P., 1957 rpt, p. 107. All the ensuing quotes from Shakespeare will be from this edition.
4. *The Two Gentlemen of Verona*, V: ii: 32-34. Craig, *op. cit.*, p. 42.
5. *Henry VI*, Pt. III, I: iii: 49-52, Craig, *op. cit.*, p. 568.
6. *Romeo & Juliet*, I: iii: 60-63, Craig, p. 769.
7. *Venus and Adonis*, Stanza I, Craig, p. 1074.
8. The last two lines of sonnet no. 18, Craig, p. 1108.
9. Craig, p. 396.
10. *Ibid.*, pp. 177-76.
11. *Ibid.*, p. 165.
12. *Ibid.*, pp. 203-04.
13. *Ibid.*, pp. 421-22.
14. *Ibid.*, p. 834.
15. *Ibid.*, p. 225.
16. *Ibid.*, p. 323.
17. *Ibid.*, p. 672.
18. *Ibid.*, p. 942.

3

A Brief Outline and a Few Relevant Facts

(A) A BRIEF OUTLINE

Macbeth is the commander of the army of King Duncan of Scotland. He, along with Banquo, another general, has come to quell the rebellion of the Thane (lord) of Cawdor. Macbeth and Banquo defeat him. Macbeth is a brave and able warrior. Quelling the rebellion was an easy task for him. The fight and the conquest are eloquently described later (*vide* Chap. 4 *infra*).

On their way back the two men pass through a heath. Here they meet the Three Witches. They can see into the future and they prophesy that Macbeth will soon became the Thane of Cowdor himself and later become the king. They also prophesy that Banquo will never become the king but he will beget a whole line of kings. At that time Macbeth and Banquo are sceptical but soon two lords enter and tell Macbeth that the king is pleased with him and has made him the thane of Cawdor. This confirmation of the witches' prophecy makes Macbeth believe in the other prophecies also and he mentally anticipates kingship. He writes the whole thing down in a letter to his wife Lady Macbeth. At almost the same time a messenger from the king comes to tell Lady Macbeth that the king is going to honour Macbeth by visiting him at his castle. It is quite natural as Macbeth is his cousin also.

Now Lady Macbeth, who has been called the fourth witch of the play is a very ambitious and forceful character. As soon as she gets Macbeth's letter she decides that he must be the king, even if they have to kill King Duncan. When the messenger tells her about the king's visit she decides that he must be killed. She has no children and is quite unscrupulous by nature.

Duncan visits Macbeth's castle with his two sons, Malcolm and Donalbain. When the king is sleeping Lady Macbeth goes quietly to kill him. She is afraid, and rightly so, that Macbeth will not be able to do so. But in actual fact it so happens that she too lacks the resolution. Duncan reminds her of her own father and she cannot lift her hand against him. So she sends Macbeth who comes back after some time, having done the deed. He has killed Duncan but at great cost to his peace of mind. From now on he hears a voice, always telling him he will not sleep any more. He is half out of his mind with anxiety and repentance. Lady Macbeth takes the bloody dagger from his hands and wipes them on the dresses of the grooms sleeping outside Duncan's room thus incriminating them. Though Macbeth is very agitated, she keeps a cool head.

Macbeth has committed three crimes in killing Duncan: regicide, killing his own cousin, and his guest, whom he ought to protect. In the morning Macduff and Lennox come to call the king as they had been requested to do. Just before they enter the castle there occurs the only comic scene in the play, "the Porter Scene" (*vide* chap. 4 *infra*). They at once find out that the king has been killed. Macbeth, showing an excess of zeal, kills the grooms. Now they cannot defend themselves. But the two sons of Duncan are not convinced of their guilt. They suspect Macbeth and fear for themselves. So they flee the country, Malcolm going to England and Donalbain to Ireland, thus leaving the kingdom free for Macbeth. He, being not only a forceful figure in the army but also the king's kinsman assumes kingship.

So the witches' prophecies are fulfilled. But there is no peace in Macbeth's mind. He knows that Banquo had heard them and that he would suspect Macbeth. Moreover, he was to sire a future line of kings. So he has to be removed if Macbeth wants to be sure of his throne. He arranges for two hired assassins to kill him and his son Fleance. This is on the same day he was to give a banquet to celebrate his accession. He has invited all the Lords, Banquo, and Fleance too.

The assassins wait for Banquo in a park nearby and attack them when they come. They kill Banquo. But Fleance manages to escape. Up till now events had gone in Macbeth's favour, but now fortune has turned against him. He does not, however, realize this. He feels that, except for Fleance, his throne is safe.

Meanwhile there is the banquet. Hypocritically, Macbeth expresses regret that Banquo is not there. This is the famous "Banquet Scene" in which he sees the ghost of Banquo. As soon as he says he is sorry at Banquo's absence he sees the ghost of Banquo sitting in his chair. He is the only one who can see the ghost. The ghost vanishes and comes again and again. Macbeth in fright shouts that he has not killed Banquo. His behavior is enough to alarm the guests. Lady Macbeth tries to control the situation by telling them that he often has such fits and gets rid of them.

Macduff, one of the lords, had suspected Macbeth and had not come to the banquet. Macbeth decides to kill him. This time Lady Macbeth turns against him. She is sick of the bloodshed and tells him she is not going to participate any more in his crimes. In the meantime, Macduff flees to England to join Malcolm. As soon as Macbeth comes to know about this he goes to Macduff's house and gets his innocent and helpless wife and children killed. His series of crimes started with Duncan. Next came the grooms and Banquo, but this is the worst crime of all. It is needless cruelty.

By now he feels the need for reassurance. So he visits the witches in their cave. In a scene fraught with awesome supernatural elements the witches make three prophecies. The first of them is that Macbeth should beware of Macduff. The second is that no one born of woman will have the power to harm him, and the third is that he will not suffer a defeat till the forest of Birnam comes to Dunsinane hill.

Up till now Lady Macbeth had been helping him in his crimes, though she had earlier said she would not do so. Now at last her sins overtake her. She starts talking and walking in her sleep, enacting the events of the night of the murder. There are three scenes in the play that need separate discussion, the

Banquet Scene, the Porter Scene and the Sleep-Walking Scene. The doctor and the maid attending to her thus come to know everything and so does everybody else.

Malcolm and Macduff reach Scotland with reinforcements from the English army. Scottish nobles meet and welcome them. Led by Malcolm they march towards Macbeth's castle in Dunsinane. He is himself there. Now Lady Macbeth is dead and life holds no meaning for him. On reaching the forest of Birnam, Malcolm orders the soldiers to cut branches from the trees and hold in front of them so as to conceal their true number. They do so. Thus, it looks as if the entire forest is marching towards Dunsinane. Macbeth sees this and realizes that the prophecy of the witches has come true.

Now he comes face-to-face with the enemy who is Macduff who has vowed to be revenged on him. He tells Macbeth that he had been "untimely ripp'd" from his mother's womb and was not born in a natural manner. This convinces Macbeth that he is facing his death. But, like the brave man that he is, he fights Macduff and is killed by him.

Malcolm succeeds to the throne and a time of peace and prosperity ensures. The tragedy of *Macbeth* comes to an end.

(B) A FEW RELEVANT FACTS

The story of *Macbeth* is historically a true one. Shakespeare had turned to Holinshed's *Chronicles* for his source material. He turned to a few other books also, particularly on witches (Scot's *Discovery of Witchcraft*, 1584). Holinshed's account of the story of Macbeth is not true in all respects, but it is known that he was really a kinsman of Duncan. He reigned for seventeen years from 1040 to 1057. He was an able and popular king and had protected his country from outside attacks. His policy with the church was a liberal one. It is said that perhaps he had even gone on a pilgrimage to Rome. But this is not sure.

The battle with Malcolm was a real one and he was killed while fighting. But it is doubtful whether the rest of the matter is historically true or not. Anyway, Shakespeare was writing a tragedy and for the sake of artistry, he had made many changes in the sources he had borrowed from.

It has been thought by scholars that the events of the play cover nine days. In brief, the scheme is:

Day 1: Act I, sc. 1-3

Day 2: Act I, sc. 4-7

Day 3: Act II, sc. 1-4
After Act II there is an interval of approximately two weeks.

Day 4: Act III, sc. 1-5
Act III, sc. 6. It is not possible to fix the time of this scene.

Day 5: Act IV, sc. 1

Day 6: Act IV, sc. 2. After this there is an interval of two weeks during which Ross comes to England.

Day 7: Act IV, sc. 3 and Act V sc. 1. After this there is an interval of three weeks during which Malcolm marches to Scotland.

Day 8: Act V, sc. 2-3

Day 9: Act V, sc. 4-8.

These are the nine days as scholars have agreed but the historical period covered is seventeen years. This covers the time from Duncan's death in 1041 to 1057 which saw Macbeth's death. Such is Shakespeare's art that an impression is given of the passing of time from Macbeth's first exuberant realization that the prophecies are true to the realization that life is a tale told by an idiot. His disillusionment is convincing as indeed is his tragic dignity. *Macbeth* is a unique play in that in this play it is the hero and not the villain who commits the crimes. It is a tragedy of darkness and this makes it all the more dark. The play from another point of view is more classical than Elizabethan as it follows the classical precept that evil characters need not lead to tragedy. This and many other issues have been endlessly debated over. What is given above is a simplified version of what has been accepted by most of the scholars. It is not necessary for students to know all arguments back and forth among them.

4

A Scene-wise Analysis

Act I, Sc. i

The first scene of any play is most important because it has many functions. It definitely sets the tone. Often it acts as a Prologue. Sometimes it introduces the main characters of the play. The first scene of *Macbeth* does the first of these because it is located on a heath with thunder and lightning and three witches. None of the dramatis personae are introduced. Instead we have the witches who influence, though indirectly, the action of the entire play. It is not that they perform any action. They just talk and decide to meet Macbeth later in the same place. They all of them chant the sinister lines:

> Fair is foul and foul is fair
> Hover through the fog and filthy air.[1]

To take up the most superficial point about the witches, there can be no question of their reality. They really exist and one proof of this is this scene. A.C. Bradley had authoritatively disposed of the theory that they are illusions:

> This supernatural element cannot in most cases if any be explained away as an illusion in the mind of one of the characters.[2]

This observation is particularly relevant for this scene for there is no other character present at all whose illusion of mind the witches can be taken to be. Yet the audience sees and hears them. So they are real.

This point settled, one can turn to other features. First of all, they set the mood of the play. Now Macbeth is well-known as the darkest of the tragedies of our poet. The witches, right from the very beginning, build the atmosphere of darkness and horror which contradicts the fact that the scene might be looked upon as grotesque. Lamb, mentioning this, asks:

> ...is the effect upon us other than the most serious and appalling that can be imagined?[3]

About the effect of the witches most critics think the same. Talking of the sources from which he took the witches, Holinshed's *Chronicles*, Schelling remarks that by his artistry Shakespeare has turned what were popular, vulgar superstitions into fearsome beings:

> ...with that imaginative freedom that transformed the vulgar, meddlesome witches of Scottish folk-lore into a supernatural embodiment of human temptation to evil.[4]

Here Schelling refers to folk-lore and Coleridge does very much the same when he compares the opening scenes of *Hamlet* and *Macbeth* and says that both of them deal with superstition. He is of the opinion that in the first this superstition is concerned with the best feelings of the human mind, and:

> ...in the second with the shadowy, turbulent and unsanctified cravings of the individual will.[5]

Both Schelling and Coleridge, it should be noted, relate the witches to the as yet undetermined desires in Macbeth's mind, though they do not deny their existence.

This is their first appearance and there will be more occasion to talk about them later. Let it be remembered that they are but only one of the manifestations of evil as well as the supernatural element in the play (*vide* analysis of IV: *infra* and others).

As an opening scene, this one is most effective. Paradoxically, it introduces characters who do not actually belong to the play, nor do they act directly. Yet it cannot be denied that as an opening scene it is most effective.

The scenes in a Shakespearean play are usually interlinked. This increases their significance and emphasizes the cohesiveness of the entire play. This scene, being the very first one is not linked to any previous scene but to the following ones. In mood, it is the precursor of the entire play and in character it is linked to the third scene of the second Act for in that scene also the witches appear. What is the most remarkable is the fact it is verbally linked to that scene also, for the words "fair" and "foul" are repeated by Macbeth right in the beginning. This kind of verbal linking is most rare.

Act II, Sc. ii

This is a much more eventful scene, though the hero is not introduced nor do any stirring events take place. But enough action is there in the speeches of the highly eloquent Sergeant who is almost unique in our poet. Duncan is there with his train and a Sergeant fresh from the battlefield enters and talks to them. He praises Macbeth to the skies and Duncan appreciates Macbeth's bravery. In poetic beauty his description is outdone by Ross who comes a little later:

> Till that Bellona's bridegroom, lapp'd in proof
> Confronted him with self-comparisons.[6]

This graphic description of Macbeth with the favourite man of the Goddess of war has made these lines famous.

Shakespeare has been praised as well as criticized for giving high-standard poetry to a mere Sergeant in this scene because the character is a mere sergeant and such poetry is out of place in his mouth. But again an artist takes all the liberties he likes if he can make them acceptable and the reader can easily accept the Sergeant as an eloquent eye-witness account of Macbeth's valour is needed here.

Act II, Sc. iii

In this scene we are once more upon the heath with the three witches. After some inconsequential talk among them that highlight their cruelty, Macbeth and Banquo enter the stage. The very first words of Macbeth recalls the closing words of sc. 1:

> So foul and fair a day I have not seen.[7]

On being addressed by Macbeth the witches hail him one by one and address him respectively as the Thane of Glamis (which he already is), Thane of Cawdor (the lord he has defeated in battle), and as Macbeth that shall be king hereafter. After this they address Banquo and tell him that he will not be the king himself, though he will sire kings. Both of them are sceptical and while they talk the witches vanish. They even think that they had been having illusions.

Then Ross and Angus enter and after duly congratulating Macbeth, tell him that the king, highly pleased with him, has made him the thane of Cawdor. Macbeth is convinced of the truth of the prophecies and at once anticipates the future:

> Two truths are told
> As happy prologues to the swelling act
> Of the imperial theme.[8]

But he is doubtful, not about the efficacy of the prophecies, but of their morality. From this moment itself he begins to hesitate, doubting and suspecting his own self. It is not surprising that critics should say that the witches do but bring to light the evil in his own mind:

> All is tumult and disorder within and without his mind....
> He is the double thrall of his passions and his evil destiny.[9]

This scene, as has been pointed out earlier, is related to the first in event, character and verbal significance. The scene started by repeating the words "fair" and "foul" when the first ended with them. This verbal echo is most uncommon. The witches appear in that scene as well as in this. Macbeth and Banquo, of course, link it to the rest of the play as far as characters go. The prophecies, needless to say, link it to the later scenes again and again as is to be expected.

Act I, Sc. iv

In this scene, Macbeth meets Duncan and the rest. Macbeth says everything that is loyal to Duncan and thanks him for the favour shown to himself. His mind, however, is full of sinister intentions of which he himself is afraid:

> Stars, hide your fires!
> Let not light see my black and deep desires.[10]

The seeds of crime are stirring within him and he is fully conscious of them.

Act I, Sc. v

In this scene, Lady Macbeth is introduced to us. Macbeth is the hero and the most important character, but Lady Macbeth is not any the less. In fact, it can be said that as a character, she is more important than Macbeth because he is like any tragic hero, after all, but she is unique and unparalleled. There is no other character like her not only in Shakespeare but in other dramatists also. Webster's heroine in *The White Devil* is sometimes given as a parallel but beside Lady Macbeth she pales into insignificance.

She enters reading the letter Macbeth has sent her. On reading the letter she at once decides that Macbeth will be king and gives a succinct analysis of his character:

> Yet do I fear thy nature;
> It is too full o' the milk of human kindness
> To catch the nearest way; thou wouldst be great,
> Art not without ambition, but without
> The illness should attend it...would not play false
> And yet wouldst wrongly win.[11]

Referring to this speech Bradley remarks that her sense of value, of morality is perverted:

> She is at once clearly distinguished from him by an inflexibility of will, which appears to hold imagination, feeling and conscience completely in check.[12]

It is not an extreme like "Evil, be thou my good" but something quite near it. As the speech develops we become aware of this, "holily" does not have for her the meaning it has for us.

While she is still brooding over all this a messenger comes from the king and tells her that he means to honour Macbeth by a visit to the castle. Then comes her invocation to the evil spirits:

> Come, you spirits
> ...Come thick night
> And pall thee in the dunnest smoke of hell
> That my keen knife see not the wound it makes.[13]

This invocation and the ones after it have made the critics call her the Fourth witch of the play.

When after this Macbeth comes and tells her about Duncan's impending visit we are not surprised at her reaction. She is determined that Duncan shall not live to see the next morning and encourages him to dissemble and act like an innocent, loyal subject.

The link of this scene with the others needs not to be explained: they are too apparent. It is linked to the former scene as well as to the latter. It is a pivotal scene.

Act I, Sc. vi

Duncan with his two sons and several lords and attendants arrives at Macbeth's castle. This scene is the only one that has a pleasant atmosphere. Duncan admires the pleasant situation of the castle and the delicate air fostered by the swallows that build their nests. Lady Macbeth comes and welcomes him. "The temple-haunting martlet" is a line often quoted by the critics. This scene is linked to the former as this visit has been mentioned earlier.

Act I, Sc. vii

Macbeth's mental torture has already begun. In this scene, we see the beginnings of it. His soliloquies in this play are no less significant than those of Hamlet. He enters to utter the first significant one of them. It has become known as containing some of the most abstract lines in Shakespeare:

> If it were done when 'tis done then 'twere well
> It were done quickly.[14]

It can be seen that in these and ensuring lines no images of any kind are there. Images come with "the bank and shoal of time" in line 6, which means that there are no less than five lines in which there are no images. So many lines free of images are difficult to find specially in our poet. They are, according to Pound, examples of logopoeia in poetry.

So Macbeth has started wondering about what is going to happen, how far he is going to succeed and what will be the further consequences of this murder even before the deed is committed. Lady Macbeth enters and with her energetic and completely unscrupulous words, whips him into action. For the time being, Macbeth is determined.

This is another decisive scene, connected both to the foregoing and ensuing scene. Almost the same thing had occurred before as the former scene also shows Macbeth hesitating and Lady Macbeth whipping him up with her tongue. The two are very much alike.

Act II, Sc. i

This is a link-scene that connects the foregoing and the ensuing ones. It is important mainly because of the supernatural element introduced in it. This time it is not the witches. It consists of a hallucination seen by Macbeth. He sees a dagger with the handle towards his hand. After some time he sees the point of the dagger dripping with blood:

> Is this a dagger which I see before me
> The handle towards my hand....
> ....or art thou but
> A dagger of the mind, a false creation
> ....I see thee still
> And on the blade and gudgeon gouts of blood
> Which was not so before.[15]

The soliloquy goes on till line 64. Maybe the dagger is as he suspects, a hallucination, "a dagger of the mind" but it is undeniable that he sees it. That is the trouble with him, the real and the unreal are so mixed up in his mind that he is extremely confused. The scene therefore serves the double purpose of being a link-scene and also of introducing a supernatural element that does not have anything to do with the witches.

Act II, Sc. ii

This is the murder-scene though the murder, as in a classical tragedy, happens off-stage. It starts with Lady Macbeth delivering a forceful speech, revealing her strong will-power. She had herself tried to go and kill Duncan but he resembled her father as he slept and she could not lift her hand against him:

Had he not resembled
My father as he slept, I
Had done't.[16]

Bradley remarks of these lines:

> They are spoken, I think, without any sentiments, impatiently, as though she regrets her weakness: but it is there.... The greatness of Lady Macbeth lies almost wholly in her courage and force of will. It is an error to regard her as remarkable on the intellectual side.[17]

Then Macbeth enters and tells her the deed is done. He is in a pitiable state of mind, hearing an invisible voice saying that he has murdered sleep and so he would sleep no more. Lady Macbeth, always practical, tells him to wash his hands and take the daggers back to the sleeping grooms. On Macbeth's saying that he cannot do so she goes to do it herself. Macbeth washes his hands and says the terrible lines:

Will all great Neptune's ocean wash this blood
Clean from my hand? No, this my hand will rather
The multitudinous seas incarnadine
Making the green one red.[18]

Act II, Sc. iii

This is the famous Porter Scene. For a long time it was thought to have been a clumsy interpolation by a hack writer who had tried to introduce some comic element into the play. Coleridge for example says:

> ...the disgusting passage of the Porter (II: 3) which I dare pledge myself demonstrate to be an interpolation of the actors.[19]

This attitude changed dramatically after the publication of De Quincey's famous essay *On the Knocking at the Gate in Macbeth*. It represents, for him, great insight in the dramatist. He concludes his essay by saying:

> Hence it is, that when the deed is done, when the work of darkness is perfect, then the world of darkness passes away like a pageantry in the clouds: the knocking at the

> gate is heard, and it makes known to the audience that the reaction has commenced, the humanity has made its reflux upon the fiendish, the pulses of life are beginning to beat again.... O mighty poet! Thy works are not as those of other men.[20]

The famous Porter Scene is not really an entire scene. It is but a speech of 24 lines by a single character, the Porter and part of a much longer scene. The Porter hears the knocking at the gate of Macbeth's castle. Actually, Macduff and Lennox have come to waken the king, for they had been asked to do so. They are knocking for admittance and the Porter chooses to think otherwise. He is very fanciful and imagines he is the Porter guarding the gates of Hell, and different sinners are coming and knocking at the gate for admittance. Every time there is knocking he imagines this. First he imagines a farmer who had expected to make quick money and unable to do so has hanged himself. He welcomes this imaginary farmer. Then when the knocking recurs he imagines that this time an equivocator, i.e. a fraud, has come and he welcomes this double-dealer. There is knocking again and this time he imagines a tailor has come who has defrauded his customers. When the knocking comes again he finally goes and opens the door.

The speech is in prose and a humorous one. The Porter jokes with each of his entrants:

> Here's a farmer that hanged himself on the expectation of plenty: come in time; have napkins enough about you, here you will sweat for't.[21]

As has been pointed out already, this cannot really be called a scene and it has no links with any other scene. It is completely independent. But it provides comic relief which is usual in Elizabethan tragedies. It is in prose, which is also right, for inferior characters or those in extraordinary situations (Lady Macbeth in the Sleep Walking Scene) were given prose.

After this Macduff and Lennox enter and Macduff goes to call Duncan and discovers the murder. Pandemonium breaks out, the alarm bell is rung. Macbeth goes to see and finds the grooms with blood-stained clothes. He kills them, pretended that he is so furious that he has killed them out of anger. After all the lords have expressed their anger and vowed revenge and gone Malcolm and Donalbain are left on the stage. They decide to go to England and Ireland respectively, there to find help.

This scene again has far-reaching consequences and is related to the foregoing and ensuing scenes very intimately.

Act II, Sc. iv

This is another link-scene. Ross and an Old Man converse and the Old Man tells of many supernatural omens he has seen, presaging bad times in future. These omens link it to the other scenes that have supernatural omens in them other than the witches.

Act III, Sc. i

Banquo, for the first time, openly mentions his suspicions of Macbeth's crime:

> Thou hast it now, King, Cawdor, Glamis, all
> As the weird women promised, and I fear
> Thou play 'dst most foully for it.[22]

He expresses the hope that the prophecies concerning him may come true also. Then Macbeth enters. He now speaks and acts like a king and tells Banquo that he is to be the chief guest in the banquet he is giving that night. Then he gets rid of everyone and says that they are free till seven at night. As soon as everyone goes out he calls the murderers he has hired and tells them what they have to do and to keep quiet about it. Both the assassins reassure him on both of these issues.

Macbeth's coolness and presence of mind has to be admired and deplored, as well as his hypocrisy. In the same scene, he honours Banquo by making him the chief guest and arranges for his murder. As yet events go in his favour but after this they will turn against him, but he does not know it yet.

This scene is linked to the third scene of Act II in which the witches had made their prophecies and it is linked to the ensuing one in which the murder takes place. It highlights Macbeth's hypocrisy.

Act III, Sc. ii

Nothing important happens in this. It is in the nature of a link-scene between two important scenes (sc. 1 and 3) in which the murder is decided and takes place respectively. Macbeth has come to be dissatisfied with what he has got, the throne, and thinks Duncan is well out of this world's affairs which are treacherous and evil. But he himself has to continue here.

Act III, Sc. iii

In this small scene of only twenty-two lines, the crucial act of the murder of Banquo takes place. The murderers attack and kill Banquo but Fleance escapes. Thus again the witches' prophecies are fulfilled. The scene is small but it is an important scene. It is connected to the scene of the prophecies, to the foregoing one and, most horrifyingly to the next one in which Banquo will appear as a Ghost. As Fleance escapes, this is the first time that Macbeth's fate turns against him. He had formerly said to Lady Macbeth "O full of scorpions is my heart" because of Banquo and more so because of Fleance, and now Fleance is the one who will live to carry on Banquo's line. There is no peace for Macbeth.

Act III, Sc. iv

This is the famous Banquet Scene. It had been anticipated in the former scene when Macbeth talked of a banquet and honoured Banquo by making him the Chief Guest. The murderers come and assure him that Banquo is killed but confess that they did not succeed with Fleance.

Macbeth meets the guests. Then comes the harrowing experience of the appearance and disappearance of the Ghost of Banquo. At first it comes and sits in Macbeth's chair and he is the only one to see it, so the others think that he is not well. After some time the Ghost disappears and Macbeth talks naturally. Then again it re-appears. This time Macbeth cannot help shouting at it:

> Avaunt! and quit may sight! Let the earth hide thee
> Thy bones are marrowless, thy blood is cold
> ....Hence, unreal shadow!
> Unreal mockery, hence![23]

Earlier he had said that he had not killed Banquo and now this! Again the ghost vanishes. Now Lady Macbeth tells the lords to go, that Macbeth is subject to such fits frequently. They go and after some talk between husband and wife the scene comes to an end.

It is one of the most famous scenes in Shakespeare and scholars have debated quite a lot over it. But they agree that the Ghost, like the witches, really exists, it is not the creation of Macbeth's imagination. He is visible only to Macbeth, but it is real for him and the audience, no hallucination. It appears twice and gestures at him ("never shake/ Thy gory locks at me") and he is terrified. However brave he is, he is no match for the insubstantial Ghost. He can fight the bear and the tiger and the rhino, but not a ghost.

One other point to be noted is that this is the last time that Lady Macbeth and Macbeth meet and talk. After this Macbeth will see her in the Sleep-walking Scene when she will not be conscious. On the stage this is their last meeting.

Act III, Sc. v

This again is another scene where the supernatural element appears in force. Not only are the witches there, but the goddess they worship, Hecate, is there also. She is angry with them and scolds them for dealing with Macbeth without consulting her. Now she tells them that she herself is going to take a hand in the affair:

> I am for the air; this night I'll speak
> Unto a dismal and a fearful end.[24]

This dreaded goddess of the witches was so much feared in those days that there are many legends attached to her. This is a link-scene preparing us for the first scene in Act IV which comes after another scene in-between.

Act III, Sc. vi

The last scene in this Act, this serves as a link between the foregoing Hecate scene and the next scene of the apparitions and visions. Lennox talks with a lord and much information is imparted here. The two lords do not suspect Macbeth. On the other hand, they praise him for having managed everything loyally and expertly. We come to know about Banquo and Fleance and Malcolm and Donalbain and Macduff. This scene, in fact, contains a summary of all that has happened up till now, but presented in Macbeth's favour. It does not carry out any important function.

Act IV, Sc. i

This is the scene in which the witches prophesy for the second time. It is a much more impressive scene and contains much more ceremony than the former one. For one thing, it has to be divided into two parts. In the first part only the witches are there and in the second part Macbeth comes. This part is the one that contains the three Apparitions.

In the first part of the scene there are the witches brewing a hellish brew in a cauldron. They chant some lines in which a list of the things boiling in the cauldron is given. Hecate comes and praises them for having been so zealous. Then she withdraws and Macbeth comes. He demands to know the answers to a few questions and there are more awe-inspiring evil rituals and then the First Apparition comes.

It is like an armed head and answers his question without even asking him. It tells him to beware Macduff and then vanishes.

The Second Apparition is more communicative. It is like a bloody child and says:

> Be bloody, bold and resolute, laugh to scorn
> The power of man, for none of woman born
> Shall harm Macbeth.[25]

Then the Third Apparition appears out of the cauldron. It is a crowned child with a tree in his hand. It speaks at length:

> Be lion-mettled, proud and take no care
> Who chafes, who frets, or which conspirers are;
> Macbeth shall never vanquished be until

> Great Birnam wood to high Dunsinane hill
> Shall come against him.[26]

So Macbeth is not only reassured but elated for what the Apparitions said made him invincible. Then there comes another show of eight kings, the last with a glass in his hand. He is followed by Banquo's ghost to show that he is their progenitor. Macbeth is most perturbed. He calls it a "Horrible sight". Seeing him so disturbed the witches try to cheer him up by song and dance and then vanish.

Then he comes to know that Macduff has gone to England. Then and there he decides to attack Macduff's castle and seize his property.

The most important feature of this scene are of course the witches. They with Hecate dominate the scene. Coleridge, with true perception, had said:

> The weird sisters are as true a creation of Shakespeare as his Ariel and Caliban.... Their character consists in the imagination disconnected from the good, they are the shadowy obscure and fearfully anomaly of physical nature, the lawless of human nature.[27]

This is their last appearance in the play. They are the beings who make us wonder whether really in his case character is destiny or not.

Act IV, Sc. ii

The scene takes place in Macduff's castle. Lady Macduff wonders at the unwisdom of Macduff in fleeing the country, leaving his family in the hands of the man he suspects of regicide. Then Ross who had been talking to her goes and a messenger comes. He warns Lady Macduff of danger and advises her to flee the place. Then he too goes and Macbeth's murderers come. They kill the son first and then pursue Lady Macduff.

The scene is further proof of the sea of crimes into which Macbeth has plunged. There is no need to kill the innocent and helpless wife and children of Macduff. This needless cruelty cannot be justified or defended in any manner. He is piling crime on crime.

Act IV, Sc. iii

Here we have left the blood-swept Scotland and come to England. The pious king Edward is on the throne and he is not one to tolerate tyranny. Macduff and Malcolm enter. The two of them have a long talk and decide to attack Scotland with England's help. Then Ross comes and tells Macduff that his castle has been attacked and his family killed. Naturally, Macduff vows to be revenged on Macbeth for this inhuman act.

This is a significant scene and a long one. It contains 239 lines and much discussion. Malcolm is humble and proclaims his inability to assume kingship. Macduff and Ross proclaim their loyalty to him as their king. We also come to know of the heaven-given healing power of King Edward and also his prophetic powers. Sponsored by such a king they feel they are protected by heaven itself. Not that any events take place in it but certain significant things happen. Both Macduff and Ross are definitely on Malcolm's side and all are ready to fight. Macbeth's end is drawing near. He has lost everyone's sympathy.

Act V, Sc. i

This is the famous Sleep-walking Scene. It has been extensively commented upon. Bradley thinks that though Shakespeare presents abnormal conditions of the mind, they do not influence the action:

> Lady Macbeth's sleep-walking has no
> influence whatever on the events that follow it.[28]

First of all it is taken to be entirely Shakespeare's own invention. There is nothing historically true about it. The entire scene is in prose. It is the only such scene. Here we see Lady Macbeth in a pitiable condition. She has broken down at last. Her misdeeds have gone back on her. Bradley has called the scene her own catastrophe.

The scene opens with a Doctor and the Gentlewoman who waits on her talking about Lady Macbeth. They have watched her for two nights but are puzzled and cannot come to any conclusions. While they are taking Lady Macbeth enters with a candle in her hand. To the horror and surprise of the Doctor she enacts the events of the night of Duncan's murder, talking in such a manner as to leave no one in any doubt as to what she is talking about. Her eyes are open but unseeing. She rubs her hands as if she is trying to clean them. Then she begins to speak. Her sentences are disjointed but the meaning is quite clear:

> ...Yet who would have thought the old man to have had so much blood in him.[29]

Then come the famous lines:

> Here's the smell of blood still: all the perfume of Arabia will not sweeten this little hand. Oh! Oh! Oh![30]

Then she seems to hear the knocking at the gate and goes to bed with Macbeth just as she had done in the murder scene. The Doctor is convinced of the crime and horrified at the result:

> Foul whisperings are abroad: unnatural deeds
> Do breed unnatural vices......
> ....
> More needs she the divine than the physician.[31]

It is a short scene, less than 90 lines long, yet its importance is extreme. It is in prose. As has been pointed out and will be again, inferior characters speak in prose and so do noble characters in extraordinary circumstances. Here Lady Macbeth is not in her right mind, so she speaks in prose.

The scene is related to the murder scene and later to the third scene in which the Doctor brings the news of her illness to Macbeth.

It is a most horrifying scene depicting for the audience a mind that is in ruins. The tragic emotions of pity and terror are most effectively evolved. This is Lady Macbeth's Last appearance on the stage. If her crime was terrible, so is her punishment now. Bradley saying that the scene shows her own catastrophe is quite right.

Act V, Sc. ii

This is a link-scene in which Scottish nobles march with their army to meet Malcolm. It serves the purpose of acquainting the audience with the fact that his own nobles are rising against Macbeth. They are all going towards Birnam.

Act V, Sc. iii

Macbeth is at his castle in Dunsinane. He is being bombarded with unwelcome reports of nobles defecting on all sides. He still pins his hopes on fearing no man born of woman and on Birnam wood coming to Dunsinane. Meanwhile the Doctor, coming from Lady Macbeth gives him his report that she is mentally sick. Then comes Macbeth's well-known speech:

> Canst thou not minister to a mind diseas'd
> Pluck from the memory a rooted sorrow
> Raze out the written troubles of the brain.[32]

The scene ends with Macbeth busily preparing for the coming battle. He prepares with courage and hope, convinced that he will not be defeated.

Act V, Sc. iv

Malcolm comes with his army to the countryside near Birnam and orders that his soldiers each carry a branch from the trees in front of him. This is in order to hide the true number of his soldiers and, all unknowing, he fulfils one of the witches' prophecies for from a distance it will look as if the forest is marching towards Dunsinane. This is actually a link-scene, linked to the foregoing and the ensuing scenes. It is also linked to the scene of the prophecies and to the next scene where Macbeth comes to know that the forest is marching towards his fort. It is a short scene, important because of the Birnam wood episode.

Act V, Sc. v

In this scene, Macbeth comes to know that the Queen is now dead. Then there comes his famous speech:

> To-morrow and to-morrow and to-morrow
> Creeps in this petty pace from day to day
> To the last syllable of recorded time.....
> .... it is a tale
> Told by an idiot, full of sound and fury
> Signifying nothing.[33]

This speech is unparalleled in its pessimism and is compared with Hamlet's "To be or not to be" speech.

Events have speeded up because directly after this speech Macbeth comes to know that the forest of Birnam is moving towards his castle. So now he knows that one of the prophecies on which he had pinned his hopes has failed him. But he is a brave warrior and an expert commander and he prepares to fight.

It should be noted that Lady Macbeth had died by her own hand, i.e. taken her own life, which is an unforgivable sin. It is a sin against God and the Holy Ghost. A suicide is denied Christian burial on consecrated ground. Shakespeare has punished no other character of his so cruelly as he has punished Lady Macbeth. He has denied her Christian burial and consigned her to damnation for all eternity. But all this will be explained later on.

Act V, Sc. vi

This is a very short (ten lines only) scene showing Macbeth preparing for the coming battle. It is only a link-scene but it does take the action forward.

Act V, Sc. vii

The end is swiftly drawing near. Macbeth is now waiting for the man that is not born of woman. He meets him in Macduff who tells him:

> Macduff was from his mother's womb
> Untimely ripp'd.[34]

Thus, two prophecies are fulfilled because one of them was that he was to beware of Macduff. Now Macbeth knows he has no hope and at first says he will not fight, but then, like the courageous man he was, decides to fight, knowing full well that he is facing certain death. They go out fighting and the killing happens off stage as is usual with classical tragedies. Thus at the last, Macbeth goes with his tragic dignity unimpaired as T.S. Eliot and several other scholars have affirmed. His courage in meeting death with dignity brings him all that he had lost when he committed crime upon crime. But now all that is forgotten and his end excites pity and terror in us.

The last speech in the play is made by Malcolm who ascends the throne. It is clear that the period of bloodshed is over and a time of peace and prosperity is about to ensure. Order is restored.

References

1. *Macbeth*, I: i; 9-10. As in the previous chapter all these and other quotations are from the Craig edn.
2. Bradley, A.C. in Bratchell, D.F. ed. *Shakespearean Tragedy*. London and New York: Routledge, 1990, p. 63.
3. Lamb, *On the Tragedies of Shakespeare* in Bratchell, *ibid.*, p. 46.
4. Schelling, F.E., *English Drama*, S. Chand and Co., 1963, p. 133.
5. Coleridge, *Lectures on Shakespeare* (1818) in Bratchell, *op. cit.*, p. 138.
6. I: ii: 55-56.
7. I: iii: 38.
8. I: iii: 127-29.
9. Hazlitt, *Characters of Shakespeare's Plays* (1817); in Bratchell, *op. cit.*, p. 137.
10. I: iv: 50-51.
11. I: v: 17-23.
12. Bradley, A.C., *Shakespearean Tragedy*. Longman, Macmillan & Co. Ltd., 1960, p. 307.
13. I: v: 41-53.
14. I: vi: 1-2.
15. II: i: 33-47.
16. II: ii: 14-15.
17. Bradley, *op. cit.*, pp. 310-11.
18. II: ii: 61-64.
19. S.T. Coleridge, *Lectures on Shakespeare* (1818) in Bratchell, *op. cit.*, p. 138.
20. Thomas De Quincey, *On the Knocking at the Gate in Macbeth* (1832) in Bratchell, p. 142.
21. II: iii: 4-7.
22. III: i: 1-3.
23. IV: i: 93-107.
24. III: v: 20-21.
25. IV: i: 79-81.

26. IV: i: 90-95.
27. Coleridge, Bratchell, *op. cit.*, p. 139.
28. Bradley, *op. cit.*, p. 62.
29. V: i: 42-44.
30. V: i: 55-57.
31. V: i: 77-81.
32. V: iii: 40-42.
33. V: v: 19-28.
34. V: vii: 44-45.

5

The Major Themes

(A) THE THEME OF GOOD AND EVIL

Tragedies always deal with the opposition of good and evil. They end with the defeat of evil and the triumph of good. But it is not as simple as it sounds. There are many side-issues connected with it and many are the arguments advanced by critics on each of these issues. It has been said by R. Ornstein that:

> We might read the progress of tragedy
> as the spiritual progress of the age.[1]

This argues that the tragic technique and tragic vision changed as the age progressed. Keeping this in mind Ornstein says that we cannot generalize about the moral vision of Jacobean tragedy. But, everything considered, he says quite firmly:

> Despite their ambiguous and imperfect ethical sympathies, the Jacobeans cherished those virtues which literature has immemorably enshrined: courage, fealty, resolution, the strength to accept and endure and the capacity to love and to sacrifice.[2]

Tragedy shows, again and again the temporary overthrowing of these virtues and the final restoration of them. Jacobean tragedy is no exception.

Aristotle, talking on the topic of thought or dianoia, insists that it expresses the moral element in the character:

> It is an expression of moral purpose, of the permanent disposition and tendency, the tone and the sentiment of the individual.[3]

So *Macbeth*, like all the tragedies, presents the subject of good and evil in various aspects though here again, there is some difference of opinion:

> Some readers will protest that Shakespeare's "solution" to the problem of evil lies not in the great tragedies but in the plays that follow.[4]

Some critics, again, say that Shakespeare's treatment of evil is more apparent in his comedies than in his tragedies. But these are opinions of an earlier age. Modern critics do not think so.

In *Macbeth*, we see a man, inherently ambitious, falling to temptation, committing crime after crime against inoffensive persons and being finally overcome by repentance and justice. The theme of good and evil has many aspects in this play. One of them, a major one, is the theme of the conflict between good and evil. This conflict also has two aspects: the outer and the inner. Outer conflict is faced by Macbeth when he faces Malcolm's army in the last Act, especially when he faces Macduff, but inner conflict is there from the very beginning. But conflict is an aspect of the plot, so it will be dealt with later (*vide* Chap. 8: The Plot, *infra*).

There are many more aspects of the problem of good and evil that involve Macbeth's character and will be discussed later (*vide* Chap. 6: The Major Characters *infra*).

(B) THE THEME OF THE SUPERNATURAL

This is one of the most important themes of the play. There is hardly any critic who has not written about this theme. It comes under two heads: (1) The three witches, (2) Supernatural phenomena other than the witches.

First of all, it is because of the supernatural elements that *Macbeth* is known as "the darkest tragedy," "the tragedy of gloom and horror". It makes Bradley say:

> Darkness, we may say blackness, broods over this tragedy.[5]

Bradley goes on to enumerate this point, quoting repeatedly from the play to give illustrations. Other critics, following him, have painstakingly counted the scenes and come to the conclusion that there are 19 scenes of darkness and seven of dusk and daylight. Bradley points out that the atmosphere of *Macbeth* is not of unrelieved black. Comparing it with *King Lear* he says it gives an impression of colour while *King Lear* is "cold gloom":

> it is really the impression of a black night broken by flashes of light and colour, sometimes vivid and even glaring.[6]

The three witches, or the weird sisters, are the most important of the supernatural elements. Some points concerning them have already been discussed in the analysis of the scenes concerning them (*vide* Chap. 4, *supra*). To sum them up, first of all one has to accept the fact that they really exist, they are not illusions in the minds of characters. It has been pointed out that in the first scene there is no other character on the stage but the audience can see and hear them. This proves they are not illusions in the mind of a character, because there are no characters to perceive them at all.

The next point is that they help in creating the mood of darkness and gloom. The audience was really frightened of them in those days. Lamb tells us that the effect they have on us is "serious and appalling". This effect is all the more remarkable because Shakespeare has taken them from ordinary Scottish folk-lore in which they are interfering vulgar creatures and he has turned them into awesome beings. This is the opinion of Schelling. Partly modifying this, Coleridge compared them with the superstitious opening scene of *Hamlet* in which, as in this, Shakespeare uses popular superstition about ghosts. Here superstition is uses to highlight the best feelings of humanity (filial duty, obedience, etc.). In this play, however, the poet makes use of superstition about the witches of highlight the worst feelings of humanity: ambition, disobedience, lack of loyalty, etc.

Most of the critics agree that the witches serve to bring the evil hidden in Macbeth's mind to the surface. Coleridge says that though they are as much a creature of the poet's mind as Ariel and Caliban are, they are more important for highlighting the evil in human nature than for anything else.

This is a rough-and-ready summing up of the points that have already been discussed but there is as yet much more to be said. There are roughly three attitudes taken up by the critics about their function in the plot: (1) That they are irrelevant and unnecessary. They carry out no necessary function in the play. (2) That they are symbolic. (3) That they control the action.

The first of these is not accepted now. The second has been accepted by many critics, Bradley being one. The third opinion is the one generally agreed upon. The chief exponent of the last two is Bradley. This is why his criticism is called "Romantic expansionist interpretation". It lays stress upon the personality of the character which is a Romantic trait and it is expansionist because it takes in many other factors. He however strongly affirms:

> The witches and their prophecies, if they are to be rationalized or taken symbolically, must represent not only the evil slumbering in the hero's soul, but all those obscurer influences of the evil in the world which hid his own ambition.[7]

Allardyce Nicoll has given a succinct summary of the critical position thus:

> Some critics believe that the witches are the evil geniuses to tempt Macbeth to his ruin. On the other hand some consider them as merely embodiments of ambitious thoughts.... Shakespeare has reconciled them with his subtle and suggestive art. The witches form the keynote, the very atmosphere of *Macbeth*.[8]

Apart from the witches there are many other manifestations of the supernatural element in the play. Taking them in order of appearance they are:

(a) the dagger Macbeth sees that he tries to clutch
(b) Banquo's ghost
(c) the portents seen by the old man in II: iv.
    A falcon towering in her pride of place
    Was by a mousing owl hawk'd and kill'd.[9]

The second most important supernatural element apart from the witches is the Ghost of Banquo. It has been discussed already in the analysis of III: iv (*vide* Ch. IV, *supra*). Bradley's view is the most authoritative and accepted one. He presents no less than six arguments for the view that it is a hallucination, only to reject most of them and comes to the conclusion now commonly accepted:

> I think that Shakespeare (1) meant the judicious to take the Ghost for an hallucination, but (2) knew that the bulk of the audience would take it for a reality and I am more sure of (2) than of (1).[10]

It should be noted that this opinion leaves one doubtful to the last: is it hallucination or is it real? What did Shakespeare mean and what exactly does Bradley mean with his (1) and (2)? It is all highly ambiguous. Things are left as they were.

(C) THE THEME OF AMBITION

One of the labels attached to *Macbeth* is that it is a tragedy of ambition. This is a fully justified description because from the very beginning we are aware of it. Macbeth himself is aware of it. He talks of "vaulting ambition", Lady Macbeth talks of his being "not without ambition" and from his speech and action this trait is fully perceptible. As soon as he finds one of the witches' prophecies fulfilled he utters the famous lines:

> Two truths are told
> As happy prologues to the swelling act
> Of the imperial theme.[11]

The imperial theme or that of ambition is more a question of character than of content because ambition can be taken to be Macbeth's tragic flaw or "hamartia" and it will be discussed when his character is being discussed (*vide* Chap. 6, *infra*). But he is not the only ambitious character in the play. His ambition is overshadowed by that of Lady Macbeth, than whom a more ambitious character is difficult to imagine. The only character who is not ambitious is Banquo and, most surprisingly, Malcolm. The latter is an unexpectedly humble character. In II: iii, talking to Macduff he displays this humility again and again. But Lady Macbeth's ambition is true enough as will be seen later.

(D) CHARACTER IS DESTINY AS THE THEME

This is a highly debatable point of view, and different critics have different opinions. It had been most succinctly expressed by Hazlitt:

> All is tumult and disorder within and without his mind... he is the double thrall of his passions and his evil destiny.[12]

This is a tricky point involving plot and character and thought, so it is expedient to say a few words about it now. It will not be necessary to quote the many arguments advanced by critics but a few of Bradley may be quoted as his view is the generally accepted one.

According to Aristotle, the thought or *dianoia* of a play is to be found in the deeds of the character. Ethos is the moral element in the character and through it (the character) ethos can find expression. It follows therefore that the thoughts and deeds of a character best express the moral purpose of a character. Ethos and dianoia both together make up a character and these are the causes of action. Both may be found in the same speech. But in a simple manner moral purpose or the determination of the will is ethos and dianoia means the intellectual aspect of the speech. But whatever the ethos or the dianoia may be they cannot exist without deed or action. Aristotle says:

> Without action there cannot be a tragedy; there may be without character.[13]

So character unites moral purpose and intellectual determination and both are subject to action. Herein the relevance of the phrase "character is destiny" becomes noticeable and related to plot or action. Everything is subjugated to action or the plot. In *Macbeth*, we find that the action or the plot always proves to us that the ethos or dianoia expressed through them tells us that so far as the hero is concerned we find that he is always conscious of what he is doing. The witches might help him to make up his mind but they do not really influence his action.

> The story or action of a Shakespearean tragedy does not consist solely of human action or deeds.... The centre of tragedy therefore may be said with equal truth to lie in action issuing from character or in character issuing in action.[14]

Or, in other words, character is destiny. Bradley considered the importance or relevance of chance or accident as a factor deciding destiny. In *Macbeth*, however, there is no question of chance taking a hand or stepping in as destiny. It may be argued that the first meeting of Macbeth with the witches that awakened his sleeping ambition was by chance so here destiny has taken a hand. It may be looked at from that point of view, but then it was Macbeth's choice after all. He acted as he did, i.e. killed Duncan because his ambition was awakened. Then later still the other murders were the result of his character, not of destiny.

These are the major themes in the play. Related to these are sub-themes like the Morality play theme, the theme that crime does not pay, Scottish history as the theme, etc. The ones mentioned above are the most important.

References

1. Ornstein, R., *The Moral Vision of Jacobean Tragedy*. The Univ. of Wisconsin Press, 1960, p. 45.
2. *Ibid*., p. 46.
3. Butcher, S.H., *Aristotle's Theory of Poetry and Fine Art*. London, Macmillan & Co., 1932, 4th ed., p. 340.
4. Ornstein, *op. cit*., p. 224.
5. Bradley, *op. cit*., p. 279.
6. *Ibid*., p. 280.
7. *Ibid*., p. 291.
8. Allardyce Nicoll, *British Drama,* 5th ed., Indian rept. 1973, New Delhi, Doaba House, p. 105.
9. II: iv: 11-12.
10. Bradley, *op. cit*., p. 426.
11. I: iii: 127-29.
12. William Hazlitt, *Characters of Shakespeare's Plays* (1817) in Bratchell *op. cit*., p. 137.
13. Butcher, *op. cit*., p. 27.
14. Bradley, *op. cit*., p. 7.

6
The Major Characters

As a creator of characters Shakespeare stands unrivalled. Not only is he a prolific writer, but he is a creator of memorable, classic characters. When a work of art can pass the test of time it can be said to have become a classic and Shakespeare's characters have not only passed the test of time, but, more than that, they have taken on an added dimension, they have become symbolic characters. It is enough for a writer to have added one or two to the gallery of characters, but he has added dozens. This has always been well-recognized. Victor Hugo had said that next to God, Shakespeare had created the most.

But mere number is not enough. What is of more importance is the quality of the characters he has created. They are not merely realistic. That is too simple a concept in relation with Shakespeare. Pope put it the best when he said, in a much-quoted sentence:

> His characters are so much Nature here that 'tis a sort of injury to call them by so distant a name as copies of her.[1]

If one looks at the different phases of his career then one finds that in the first phase of his apprenticeship the characters most of the time are rather superficial ones. There are no memorable characters in the plays of that time. But things changed with the second phase. He was learning at a prodigious rate, and it shows in his characters. Even in the early part of Phase II we have memorable characters, particularly that of Bottom while in the later stage, with the Golden Comedies, he has come into his own with his inimitable heroines. He excels, by this time, in male as well as female characters. If there is Rosalind on one hand, there is Shylock on the other.

Then comes Phase III and the Four Great Tragedies. All the four tragic heroes were created at this time. It has been remarked that tragedies are there in Phase I and II also, e.g. Romeo in Phase I and Julius Caesar in II. But Romeo does not come up to the standards of a Hamlet or an Othello, though he has become the archetype of the star-crossed lover. *Julius Caesar*, though a tragedy, does not really have a tragic hero as such for Caesar is there for a very short time and cannot really be called the ideal tragic hero. For that we have to come to the Four Great Tragedies and to them only, for after them we no longer have tragedies. *Antony and Cleopatra* and *Coriolanus* are two late tragedies and here too we have great characters in the person of the tragic hero who fulfill all the classical requirements. All the same, the four great heroes, Hamlet, Othello, Lear, and Macbeth stand by themselves, towering over the others. They have attained the status of universality and therefore are the "concrete universals".

Shakespeare had not only real life but many other supporting elements to fall back upon when creating his characters. There were the classical theories and examples from Seneca and the others among the ancients as well as contemporary customs and stage conventions, not to mention the native mediaeval plays like the Moralities. *Macbeth* indeed has been called a Morality play. Rules for the writing of plays had been clearly formulated by Aristotle and his commentators. It has been already pointed out (*vide* Chap. 3 *supra*) he had studied Plautus and Terence in comedy and Seneca in school. In addition to these many other works by contemporary writers on the subject of characters were available, as Thomas Newton's *The Touchstone of Complexions*, Bishop Hall's *Characters of Virtues and Vices*, Overbury's *Characters*. These later books contained sketches of characters too. Theophrastus's well-known book which had been translated by Boyes contained more than a hundred of such character-sketches to help the dramatist. This had classical precedent because Aristotle himself had given character-sketches in his *Ethics* where there are pages and pages devoted to this topic. In addition in *Poetics* he had given clear-cut rules concerning dramatic characters at which we will have a look now.

According to Aristotle, all dramatic characters, whether tragic or comic, should have four qualities: (1) Proportion, (2) Appropriateness, (3) Realism, and (4) Consistency. The first of these is intimately concerned with ethos, for it has two implications. First of all another name he gives for it is Goodness and says that the moral intention of the person must be good:

> Any speech or action that manifests moral purpose of any kind will be expressive of character: the character will be good if the purpose is good.[2]

Aristotle had a very practical mind and pointed out this goodness differs from person to person. The example he gives is that of a servant. If a servant refrains from theft that will be goodness in him, but in a person of a higher class it will be taken for granted, without any moral value.

The second implication of goodness is that it must exist, not in a pure form, unadulterated by any badness, for it would not be lifelike. Goodness must be mixed with evil as in real life.

The second quality demanded by Aristotle in a character is that of Appropriateness. A person should speak and act like the person he is, in accordance with his position in society. He gives an example so as to clarify this point:

> There is a type of manly valour, but valour in a woman or unscrupulous cleaverness is inappropriate.[3]

Generally speaking, there is no violation of this rule in our poet. His characters usually speak or behave in accordance with their station in life. But the play under discussion contains two characters that are exceptions. The first is the sergeant who gives the information about the battle in Act II, sc. ii. He speaks most eloquently, unlike a soldier. As has been pointed out in the relevant place, Shakespeare has been criticized for putting poetry of a high order in the mouth of an ordinary soldier. The second exception is, of course, Lady Macbeth. Her entire character is a violation of the rule of appropriateness as will be discussed later.

The third characteristic demanded by Aristotle is realism. Unfortunately, he does not write at length about this point. This rule is definitely observed by our poet. Pope's observation given above is ample proof of it. His characters always act true to life and to themselves. Again in our play there is the example of Lady Macbeth. She may not be a realistic character but she is true to life. On the other hand, the only other female character Lady Macduff is a fully realistic character. She talks indulgently to her little son, is critical of her husband, and, faced by danger, succumbs to it. She is one's idea of a perfectly normal woman.

The fourth quality of consistency is the most important of the four. It implies that the character must remain true to its own nature. Macbeth is presented as an ambitious man and remains so to the end. This does not mean that the character must remain unchanged because that again would not be realistic. Subtle changes will occur in a character according to change in circumstances but they should be such as to be acceptable, he must be recognizably the same person. In addition to being ambitious, Macbeth is also presented as a person who is full of doubts and hesitations and he remains the same till the very end. From "If it were done" to his hesitation to fight Macduff on being told of his unnatural birth he acts true to his nature.

With the classical rules on one hand and contemporary examples on the other Shakespeare had much to observe and much to deviate from. Indeed, every one of the dramatists had the same. Yet it was Shakespeare who has given us a full gallery of immortal characters. H. Fluchère, stressing this aspect, says:

> It is equally undeniable that, allowing for his own peculiar genius, he conforms with the accepted conventions of character-drawing as with other conventions.[4]

When we come to the tragic hero, then, in addition to these we find another set of rules given by Aristotle. Again, Shakespeare had the example of the heroes of Kyd and Marlowe before him. Formidable examples which, nevertheless, he overcame and triumphed over.

The most important rules about the tragic hero as given by Aristotle are:

(1) The hero must be noble by birth.

(2) He must be noble by nature too.

(3) He must have a flaw in him.

The third of these is the most important, and has come to be known as the "tragic flaw" or "hamartia" that brings about his tragic doom upon him. It does not mean a serious moral flaw. Aristotle says of the tragic hero:

> A man who is not eminently good and just, yet whose misfortune is brought about not by vice or depravity but by some error or frailty.[5]

Thus, it is an error, not a serious flaw that brings about tragic doom: hesitation in Hamlet, jealousy in Othello, ambition in Macbeth. The man is essentially a noble one, but he goes on making mistakes, Macbeth more so than the others because he piles crime upon crime and loses the sympathy of the audience. At last, of course following the stoical tradition set by Seneca he recovers his courage and faces death right nobly, thus retrieving his tragic dignity and exciting pity and terror in our heart. But it has to be remembered that the tragic character is above the average and in depicting him the dramatist "should present the type and yet ennoble it".

In a tragedy, the character of the hero is of such overwhelming importance that often he is the only major character in a play. But that is not the case with *Macbeth*. Here Lady Macbeth is of equal, if not more, importance. The characters of Banquo and Macduff should also be treated as major ones.

Macbeth

Macbeth as the tragic hero overshadows all other characters in the play, though in this play an exception has always to be made in the case of Lady Macbeth. Macbeth, however tremendous a personality he has, does fall rather low as a tragic hero when he piles crime upon crime and specially when he has Lady Macduff and the children killed. Let us, however, proceed according to the rules given by Aristotle.

The first two requirements of the Aristotelian hero are easily fulfilled. Macbeth is both noble by birth (he is the king's kinsman). Aristotle had said concerning this point:

> He must be one who is highly renounced and prosperous—a personage like Oedipus, Theyestes or other illustrious men of such families.[6]

Macbeth is definitely all this, belonging to a high family, the royal family of Scotland. He is also noble by nature though this second trait becomes more and more qualified as the play progresses. But from the very beginning there is no doubt about his nobility as a warrior. Apart from the Sergeant's awestruck presentation of his valour, there is the unforgettable description of Ross, instinct with lyrical beauty:

> Till that Bellona's bridegroom, lapp'd in proof
> Confronted him with self-comparisons.[7]

Valour mixes here with beauty that he can be imagined as being the favourite of the goddess of war. We know of many human beings loved by goddesses and they were noted for beauty (Aurora–Tithonus, Venus–Adonis, Venus–Anchises) but that a soldier should for his valour be imagined as the beloved of a goddess argues for beauty of a different kind.

This nobility is one which he retains to the last. In fact at the end it is through this that he recovers his tragic dignity. It is true that he does not personally kill any of his victims (except Duncan), getting them killed by assassins and thus trying to get rid of the moral responsibility ("Thou canst not say I did't"). In the ideal tragic hero, as Aristotle says:

> An imitation of persons who are above the common level.... The poet, in representing men who are irascible, or indolent, or have other such defects of character, should present the type and yet ennoble it.[8]

So here Shakespeare has presented a character who is definitely above the common level and though the type is that of ambitious men, has ennobled it.

Now the third point about the ideal tragic hero is that of "hamartia" which actually means to miss the mark in archery. Aristotle is careful to make it clear that it is an "error in judgement" not a serious flaw:

> A man who is not eminently good and just, yet whose misfortune is brought about not by vice or depravity but by some error or frailty.[9]

This "error or frailty" had been taken as a fatal flaw by the Elizabethans in whose plays it leads to crime as it did not in Greek plays. Oedipus made many mistakes but killing (except for the first time) was not one of them. But here Shakespeare had yielded to contemporary custom and made Macbeth a criminal which is un-Aristotelian. It was no error of judgement that made him kill Duncan but cold calculated premeditation. The same, even more so, was the case with Banquo and the others, culminate in the murder of Lady Macduff and her children.

Theodore Spencer points out that in the course of *Macbeth*, the main character develops the bad qualities:

> Macbeth grows into evil; that is why those critics are right who describe the play as a more intense study of evil than any other.[10]

He points out that at the beginning of the play the hero:

> ...is like the weather, both fair and foul—neither one nor the other, and with potentialities for either. The witches... send him towards evil as does his wife.[11]

Sent towards evil, he commits the crimes and becomes the king. He becomes the king only to satisfy ambition. Never does he give evidence of the responsibilities of kingship. These were realized well enough in those days—a king had duties as well as privileges. St. Thomas Aquinas, commenting on the position of the king said:

> Therefore let the king realize that such is the office which he undertakes, namely, that he has to be in the kingdom what the soul is in the body and what God is in the world.[12]

Everyone was well aware of the sacred nature of a king, that his person is sacrosanct, "the Lord's anointed temple". But to Macbeth the throne is but something to take advantage of, for self-aggrandisement, not to give service to a greedy and selfish attitude, the opposite of Malcolm's.

This is a far more sensitive and perceptive view than the one that finds Macbeth steeped in crime from the beginning. It is more sensitive to perceive that it was not so from the beginning but that Macbeth became more and more evil as the play progressed.

If we turn now to the other four traits given by Aristotle: Proportion, Appropriateness, Realism and Consistency we will find that Macbeth conforms to them. The first of them is his weakness because of the moral part of it. Macbeth's intention, from the very beginning, is evil rather than good. The second point is in better conformity with his nature. It implies that in a character good and evil must be in proper proportion. The character must not be totally good nor totally bad. This is more or less true of Macbeth because he is a valiant man, respected by all. The bad qualities, as Spencer has said, develop gradually in him.

As for appropriateness, this is not a point to be laboured over. Macbeth always says and does what is proper, and often this makes him hypocritical. Two notable instances of this are (1) when he professes loyalty and gratitude to Duncan while contemplating murdering him, and (2) when he honours Banquo while planning to kill him. The only places where he acts unnaturally are when he sees the Ghost of Banquo in the Banquet Scene. Here his behavior is manifestly unnatural, most unlike a king who is hosting a banquet.

Yet when we come to Realism even his behavior in the Banquet Scene can be defended. As it is, his behavior is realistic all the time. This becomes the most remarkable when he enters the stage for the first time as a king. How easily he takes on the speech and manner of a king, as if he were born to it! His behavior when he sees the Ghost is perfectly natural and realistic when we consider the circumstances. To everyone else he is behaving unnaturally but the audience cannot see the Ghost and therefore to them his behavior to perfectly realistic. In fact, it would have been unnatural if he had been calm and unperturbed. Nothing is more natural for him than to cry out:

> Avaunt! and quit my sight! Let the earth hide thee
> Thy bones are marrowless, thy blood is cold
> ....Hence, unreal shadow!
> Unreal mockery, hence![13]

Realism is also in evidence when he hears about Lady Macbeth's death. He is busy preparing for the coming battle. The man who was terrified of the consequences of his deed has vanished, the efficient commander has taken over. He has no time to sit down and mourn. But life has become meaningless for him. The famous speech comes, comparing life to a nonsensical tale:

> ...it is a tale
> Told by an idiot, full of sound and fury
> Signifying nothing.[14]

Right after this he plunges back into work. No sentimentality is there. There is no time for him to indulge in it and this is perfectly natural and realistic. The meaninglessness of life is most superbly conveyed in a few lines and so is his grief. Had he given up preparing for battle and started to mourn, that would have been unrealistic for him.

Finally, we come to the quality of consistency. Aristotle lays great stress on it. A character must behave in a way that is consistent with his nature. This does not mean that the character must not change. But the change should come gradually so that the character remains recognizably the same as he had been in the foregoing scenes. Aristotle gives so much importance to this attribute that he says if a character is portrayed as inconsistent "he must be consistently inconsistent". This is seen in the fact that there is one trait in his nature: his not hesitating but speculating as to what is to happen after he has killed Duncan. It is the most evident in the speech:

> If it were done when 'tis done, then 'twere well
> It were done quickly.[15]

Then, thinking of the heinousness of his crime he thinks nothing will clean his hand:

> Will all great Neptune's ocean wash this blood
> Clean from my hand? No, this my hand will rather
> The multitudinuous seas incarnadine
> Making the green one red.[16]

After the deed is done, in the course of the play he repeatedly expresses doubt and repentance for the crime, going so far as to envy Duncan for being well out of this treacherous world:

Duncan is in his grave:
After life's fitful fever, he sleeps well,
Treason has done his worst; nor steel nor poison
Malice domestic, foreign levy, nothing,
Can touch him further.[17]

This kind of attitude to his crime and to his own psychological condition—self-condemnatory, doubtful, vacillating, is something that endures till the end. Herein we find consistency in him, herein is he "consistently inconsistent" because he never stops doubting.

Thus on all counts we find that Macbeth fulfills all the classical requirements of the ideal tragic hero. On contemporary counts also, he can be taken to be the type of Ambitious man and the Senecan hero. He himself and his critics recognize the ambitious element in himself. This has already been discussed. The Senecan element remains to be pointed out. It was present there in contemporary drama and of course, in the tragedies of Seneca that he had studied. Kyd's and Marlowe's plays present ample examples. But Senecan heroes were not only dignified and endured suffering stoically. There is an element of self-dramatization that T.S. Eliot has pointed out:

It is the attitude of self-dramatization
assumed by some of Shakespearean
heroes at moments of tragic intensity
...only Shakespeare does it both more
poetically and more lifelike.[18]

This trait of self-dramatization is very much there in Macbeth. It is not much in evidence in his last speech which is remarkable, not for its self-dramatization but for other Senecan qualities like facing death with courage:

I will not yield
To kiss the ground before young Malcolm's feet
And to be baited with the rabble's curse.
Though Birnam wood be come to Dunsinane
And thou oppos'd, being of no woman born
Yet I will try the last. Before my body

I throw my warlike shield: lay on Macduff
And damn'd be him that first cries "Hold, enough".[19]

This is Stoicism at its most sublime—facing certain death with courage. Macbeth is the most ideal tragic hero created by Shakespeare. In fact, the word "Sublime" has been used repeatedly by Bradley with reference to the play and it is the hero who gives it this sublimity.

Lady Macbeth

Lady Macbeth is a unique character, not only in Shakespeare but in the literature of all time. She has often been compared with Vittoria Corrombona of Webster's *The White Devil*, but actually Vittoria is but a rather ill-intentioned character at best in comparison with Lady Macbeth. She does not exude the aura of evil as Lady Macbeth does. Bradley sums up the critical opinion:

> Shakespeare meant the predominant impression to be one of awe, grandeur and horror and that he never meant this impression to be lost.[20]

It is true that Malcolm calls her the "fiend-like queen" and Dr. Johnson declares that Lady Macbeth "is merely to be detested", but the modern critics agree in allowing her the quality of grandeur, of tragic dignity, of being able to excite pity and terror.

Right from the very beginning we can see that Shakespeare lays stress on the attributes in her character that inspire awe and a feeling of unnaturalness. Her reaction on reading the letter can be taken as the loyal zest of a loyal wife, but the terrible invocation later to the evil spirits cannot be looked upon in that way:

Come you spirits
That tend on mortal thoughts, unsex me here
And fill me, from the crown to the toe, top-full
of direst cruelty....
.......come to my woman's breasts
And take my milk for gall
......come thick night
And pall thee in the dunnest smoke of hell
That my keen knife see not the wound it makes.[21]

No wonder Bradley said "the witches are nothing to her" and "though she is terrible she is also sublime" (*op. cit.*, p. 277). She would certainly inspire terror in the heart of the Elizabethan audience and they would whole-heartedly agree that she is the fourth witch of the play.

This desire to go against nature manifests itself again later when she tells Macbeth of suckling a baby:

> I would, when it was smiling in my face
> Have plucked my nipple from his boneless gums
> And dashed the brains out, had I so sworn as you.[22]

It is this desire to be unfeminine that would have terrified an Elizabethan audience, it is so much against nature.

After she has lashed Macbeth with her tongue and whipped him into action we see her next on the night of the murder. Here she voices the one evidence of weakness in her character:

> Had he not resembled
> My father as he slept, I had done't.[23]

This might be taken as a redeeming feature or one of human weakness in her character. But Bradley thinks not:

> They are spoken, I think, without any sentiment, impatiently as though she regretted her weakness.[24]

What Bradley says might well be true, who knows what Shakespeare had intended? Anyway, after this we see her well recovered from this momentary weakness and, realizing the condition of her husband, herself doing the needful, i.e. taking the bloody dagger to the grooms and wiping it on their dress. Later when she comes back after she has done it her attitude is still practical and eminently unsentimental when Macbeth thinks that whole oceans will not clear his hand she says:

> A little water clears us of this deed
> How easy is it then?[25]

Then, trying to instill courage into her husband she retires with him to bed. She is full of common sense after these uncommon happenings but we know how terribly she will have to pay for this common sense in the sleep-walking scene.

After this we see her when the murder is discovered and she pretends to faint with shock and is carried out. Next we see her in the Banquet scene where she is her efficient, practical self, managing an awkward situation with great presence of mind:

> Sit, worthy friends: my lord is often thus
>
> And hath been from his youth Pray you keep your seat
> The fit is momentary.
>
> ....
>
> I pray you speak not: he gets worse and worse
>
> Questions enrage him; at once good night...go at once.[26]

Here she is eminently self-controlled but hereafter her punishment starts. On the stage this is the last time she is fully in command of herself. After this we see her in the sleep-walking scene. Bradley comments:

> The sleep-walking scene again inspires pity but its main effect is one of awe...there is no trace of contrition...she is too great to repent.[27]

There are three assertions here and all are true in relation to Lady Macbeth. Her condition inspires more fear than pity in us, she is re-living that terrible night, but there is no trace of repentance in her. Indeed, she is not conscious at all so that the question of repentance does not arise. Finally, she is too great to repent—this is also true. In the presentation of her character we have seen many attributes, but humility is not one of them and humility is essential for repentance.

When enacting the events of that fateful night she says most revealing and incriminating things. The most famous of her speeches is the one about perfumes of Arabia:

> Here's the smell of blood still: all the perfumes of Arabia will not sweeten this Little hand. Oh! Oh! Oh![28]

This is her last appearance on the stage. Next we hear of her death. Bradley calls this scene her own catastrophe.

The manner of her death is not clarified till much later. In his speech, Malcolm says:

> by self and violent hands
> Took off her life.[29]

Some points about her death had been mentioned before but they are so important as to need repetition. It should be remembered that in making her kill herself Shakespeare has punished her far more terribly than he has any other character. According to Christianity, suicides are eternally damned. For all other sins there is hope that one day, after due purgation they will be saved, but never a suicide. A suicide is not allowed to be buried in the burial place of a church because it is consecrated ground. Instead he is buried in cross-roads. All Christians have a cross erected on their tomb, but not a suicide. He has a stake driven through his heart. All these were facts well-known to the Elizabethan audience. This added to the effect of terror excited by hero.

Her uniqueness as a character need not be pointed out. What has to be stressed is the fact that in the play itself, actually she is more important than Macbeth himself. This is because Macbeth, when all is said and done is after all another tragic hero among many. But Lady Macbeth is unique. There is no one like her. As Bradley says "though she is terrible she is also sublime." Sublimity apart, she stands alone in her uniqueness. No one can approach her. She has been tentatively compared with Webster's heroine in *The White Devil* as has already been mentioned. But in her aura of evil and grandeur Vittoria Corrombona cannot approach her. *Macbeth* is a play in which paradoxically the tragic hero is of less importance than the heroine. In this play, the heroine rivals the tragic hero is importance.

Banquo

Banquo's character may not look very important at first. In fact as a Ghost he is of more importance than as a live man, but he is the next major character after the hero. Bradley is of the opinion that it is in the changes he undergoes and the influence of the witches that his interest lies and readers most of the time do not realize that this was Shakespeare's intention. On the other hand, most people look upon him as a foil to, a contrast to Macbeth as innocence versus guilt. Bradley agrees with this but with reservations:

> ...it seems to be supposed that this must be continued till his death; whereas in reality, though it is never removed, it gradually diminishes.[30]

Bradley therefore makes several statements about Banquo: (1) he undergoes some changes, (2) the witches influence him, (3) he is a contrast to Macbeth, (4) this contrast is gradually diminished. Then he proceeds to prove these assertions by following Banquo's "story".

When they meet the witches, he is not apprehensive about them. Bradley thinks him to be a bold man as he addresses them without any fear and has no feeling of guilt. When they vanish he is surprised and says that they might be products of imagination. When later Macbeth reminds him of the prophecy that his children will be kings he answers lightly enough to make it clear he does not attach much importance to the prophecies. Here the poet is indebted to Holinshed:

> Banquo jested with him and sayde, now Macbeth thou haste obtayned those things which the twoo former sisters prophesied, there remayneth onely for thee to purchas that which the third sayd should come to passe.[31]

He acts throughout in a manner thoroughly unaware of any significance in Macbeth's behavior though he notices that he is "rapt". Bradley specially points to the "thought martlet" speech to highlight the fact that there is no secretiveness in him. He speaks in a perfectly frank manner.

Then things start getting serious. Banquo is uneasy at getting Macbeth's summonses:

> A heavy summons lies like lead upon me
> And yet I would not sleep.[32]

His attitude undergoes a marked change in the murder scene. On being told of the murder he tersely remarks: "Too cruel anywhere" and probably he suspects the truth, then and there. After sometime he speaks in a language that is solemn and most unlike him:

> Fears and scruples shake us:
> In the great hand of God I stand, and thence

> Against the undivulged pretence I fight
> Of treasonous malice.[33]

The formality of tone and solemnity of language leaves us in no doubt that there are grave doubts in his mind, if not certainties.

But nothing significant happens. When we see him next he is gratefully accepting Macbeth's invitation to be the chief guest at a banquet and Bradley thinks that he has accepted Macbeth's crime and acquisces in it because he hopes that the prophecies concerning him may be fulfilled too. When Macbeth kills Banquo it is a changed Banquo:

> But the Banquo he kills is not the innocent soldier who met the witches and daffed their prophecies aside.[34]

Bradley does not analyse his character any further. He does not develop or discuss any of the points mentioned earlier by him, of Banquo's being a contrast, etc. as mentioned earlier. A more detailed analysis is awaited.

Macduff the Thane of Fife

Macduff the thane of Fife is another major character in the play, though Bradley does not consider him to be so, nor do the others. But he is not only the leader of those who oppose Macbeth but the one to kill him. At least for that reason, if for no other, he is one of the major characters.

We see him first when he enters at the end of the Porter Scene. It is he who had been knocking at the gate. He has come to call the king because he had been asked to do so. He goes to waken the king and at once discovers the murder. He cries out:

> Most sacrilegeous murder hath broken ope
> The Lord's anointed temple and stole thence
> The life of th' building.[35]

At once alarm spreads. He wakens everyone. As yet he has no suspicion of Macbeth. Perhaps it enters his head when Macbeth kills the grooms but in this scene there is no inkling of any suspicion. Nor is any hint of it given in the scene with the Old Man. In the Banquet Scene, he is absent because he is already suspicious and we come to know from the talk between Lennox and the Lord that he has gone to England to join Malcolm.

In IV: iii we see him with Malcolm in England. Many things about him become clear in the long conversation they have. First of all there is his patriotism:

Bleed, bleed, poor country
Great Tyranny, Lay thou thy basis sure
For goodness dare not check thee.[36]

His suspicion of Macbeth is also clear:

Nor in the legions
Of horrid hell can come a devil more damn'd
In evils to top Macbeth.[37]

He declares his loyalty to Malcolm as the rightful king of Scotland. Then Ross comes and he asks about his wife and children. At first Ross tells him that they are safe. But after some time he tells the terrible truth that Macbeth has killed all his family:

All my pretty ones
Did you say all? O hell-kite! All?
What, all my pretty chickens and their dam
At one fell swoop?[38]

This sets him revengefully, against Macbeth. Before this it was patriotism and loyalty, but now personal enmity is added to his other feelings:

Bring thou this fiend of Scotland and myself;
Within my sword's length set him, if scape
Heaven forgive him too.[39]

Already Macbeth knows, by this time, that he has to beware the thane of Fife. Macduff is now his deadly enemy.

We see him next at the battlefield. He is vengefully looking for Macbeth with death in his heart. Now patriotism and loyalty are swept aside as personal wrongs have taken over:

My wife and children's ghosts will haunt me still.
......either thou Macbeth
Or else my sword with unbatter'd edge
I sheathe again in undeeded.[40]

Then comes the last, the crucial scene. Macbeth still has the assurance of not being harmed by man born of woman and now he tells this to Macduff:

> Thou losest labour
> I bear a charmed life which must not yield
> To one of woman born.[41]

He thinks this would dismay Macduff. On the other hand, it gives the latter new assurance and confidence that he is certainly going to win:

> Macduff was from his mother's womb
> Untimely ripp'd.[42]

He next enters, triumphant, with Macbeth's head. Now that vengeance is satisfied, patriotism and loyalty take over:

> Hail King, for so thou art,
> Behold where stands
> The usurper's head, the time is free
> ....
> Hail King of Scotland.[43]

This is the career of Macduff an honourable one it is.

He is loyal as well as patriotic, valorous, and noble. Though Bradley and the other critics do not consider him as a major character he is definitely one and has been carefully portrayed, like all the characters of Shakespeare.

References

1. Quoted by Fluchère, H., *op. cit.*, p. 131.
2. Butcher, S.H., *op. cit.*, p. 53.
3. *Ibid.*, p. 53.
4. Fluchère, *op. cit.*, p. 136.
5. Butcher, *op. cit.*, p. 45.
6. *Ibid.*, pp. 45-47.
7. I: ii: 55-56.
8. Butcher, *op. cit.*, p. 57.
9. *Ibid.*, p. 45.
10. Spencer, T., *Shakespeare and the Nature of Man*, Cambridge, at the Univ. Press, 1945, p. 153.

11. *Ibid.*, p. 157.
12. *Ibid.*, p. 17.
13. IV: I: 93-107.
14. IV: v: 26-28.
15. I: vii: 1-2.
16. II: ii: 61-64.
17. III: ii: 21-25.
18. Eliot, T.S. *Selected Essays, The Stoicism of Seneca*, 1932, Faber and Faber.
19. V: viii: 28-34.
20. Bradley, *op. cit.*, pp. 273 and 317.
21. I: v: 40-50.
22. I: vii: 55-57.
23. II: ii: 14-15.
24. Bradley, *op. cit.*, p. 310.
25. II: ii: 66-67.
26. III: iv: 33-35, III: iv: 116-19.
27. Bradley, *op. cit.*, p. 318.
28. V: i: 55-57.
29. V: iii: 69-70.
30. Bradley, *op. cit.*, p. 319.
31. Quoted in *ibid.*, p. 322, footnote.
32. II: I: 8-9.
33. II: iii. 109-12.
34. Bradley, *op. cit.*, p. 325.
35. II: iii: 50-53.
36. IV: iii: 30-32.
37. IV: iii: 54-56.
38. IV: iii: 211-14.
39. IV: iii: 228-30.
40. V: vii. 15-20.
41. V: vii: 9-14.
42. V: viii. 14-15.
43. V: viii. 53-59.

7

The Minor Characters

There are many dramatists who take care over their major characters but not over their minor ones. Marlowe is an extreme example for whom minor characters, as it were, did not exist. Shakespeare is never like others. His minor characters also are delineated with loving care. Even if a character comes only for a short time on the stage he is portrayed convincingly. The present play contains one famous example of an extremely minor one who comes on the stage only once and yet is portrayed with extraordinary depth and feeling. It is, of course, the Sergeant who comes in sc. ii of Act I who has been mentioned already. But apart from him the other minor characters too are carefully portrayed. Some of them will be considered now. They will be taken up according to the List of the Dramatis Personae as given in the text. Only a few will be taken up, not all of them.

Duncan

Duncan the king of Scotland, is a benevolent character, beloved of all. The way he reacts to the Sergeant's description of the battle and Macbeth's valour is typical. Duncan is proud of Macbeth and highly appreciative. He is the first to voice his admiration:

> O valiant cousin! Worthy general![1]

As soon as he comes to know from Ross about the capture of the thane of Cawdor he quickly gives the title to Macbeth:

> What he hath lost noble Macbeth hath won.[2]

When in Act I sc. iv Macbeth comes he is not niggardly in his praise:

Only I have left to say
More is thy due than more than all can pay.[3]

But it is not that though he praises Banquo also he rewards him also. All the rewards are for Macbeth. Perhaps this is because Macbeth is his own cousin. He repeats the word "kinsman" again and again.

He decides to honour Macbeth by paying him a visit. It was a signal honour to receive a visit from the king, though for a day only. Here the king decides to spend the night at Macbeth's castle—a proof of the trust he places on Macbeth. Lady Macbeth is fully aware of the honour and receives him gracefully when he comes. After praising the situation of Macbeth's castle Duncan once more expresses his approval of Macbeth, telling Lady Macbeth:

Conduct me to mine host, we love him dearly.
And shall continue our graces towards him.[4]

Unfortunately, this is the last time he is on the stage. He appears only for a few scenes, speaks and acts benevolently. There is not the least touch of envy or malice in him. He is eminently a good king, giving praise and rewards where they are due. This is what makes Macbeth's crime all the more heinous: that he kills a person who is all goodness and benevolence, specially towards him.

Malcolm

Malcolm, the elder of the two sons of Duncan is the next on the list. He appears on the stage quite a few times and impresses us by his foresight as well as humility. As soon as he hears that Duncan is murdered he knows he and his brother are in danger. The fiction that the grooms have killed does not convince him at all. He suspects foul play at higher level. Donalbain spells it out for him.

The near in blood, the nearer bloody.[5]

Up to now, in these few lines we come to know of him as a young man with foresight, the ability to take the right decision quickly and to act on it quickly—all admirable qualities. We come to know him far better in the long scene in England (IV: iii) when he talks with Macduff. He is not sure of Macduff's loyalty so he cannot speak very frankly which he acknowledges a bit later:

> ......crave your pardon
> That which you are, my thoughts cannot translate
> Angels are bright still, though the brightest fell.[6]

Then Macduff says "I am not treacherous" and he speaks more frankly. This caution shows circumspection in him. Then we come to know another admirable trait in him. It is humility which can be taken to be a lack of confidence in himself. It can be looked at both ways so let us regard it as humility. He thinks he is not fit to be king:

> It is myself I mean: in what I know
> All the particulars of vice so grafted
> ....
> And my desire
> All continent impediments would o'erbear
> That did oppose my will. Better Macbeth
> Than such an one to reign.
> ....
> The king-becoming graces
> As justice, verity, temperance, stableness
> Bounty, perseverance, mercy, lowliness
> Devotion, patience, courage, fortitude,
> I have no relish of them.[7]

All this is really very fine. It proves that he has humility, though it is rather exaggerated. He sees himself temperamentally unfit to rule but he takes rather an extreme view of this unfitness. That is why it was observed that this can be looked upon negatively—as lack of confidence. Thereafter, however, after Macduff has spoken he becomes more optimistic and says he will do his best to be a good king, unfit though he might be:

> God above
> Deal between thee and me, for even now
> I put myself to thy direction.[8]

Once he has taken the decision to assume kingship he changes. It is a subtle change but fully credible and admirable. He now assumes command and issues orders. In IV: ii he has come with his army to Birnam and here, in order to conceal the true number of his soldiers he orders them each to carry a branch in front of him. It was a practical order out of a practical motive but by chance he fulfilled one of the witches' prophecies. This proves that he was lucky, beloved of the gods. These things mattered in those days. Then in V: vi he shows himself well able to assume command as he ordered his uncle and Macduff what to do. Then in his last speech he is a full-fledged king, aware of his duties and privileges and one is sure that a time of peace and prosperity is going to come.

Malcolm, thus, though a minor character, is an extraordinarily well-drawn one, a fully three-dimensional being. He develops from a young man to a full-fledged king, just and powerful but never is the change a surprising one. As a character he is as carefully drawn as a major character. There is the same painstaking care.

Ross

Ross is another nobleman who plays a significant part, coming repeatedly on the stage. He comes first in I: ii just after the Sergeant has left. He brings the news of Macbeth's triumph in the battlefield. It is he who gives the lyrical description of Macbeth:

> Till that Bellona's bridegroom, lapp'd in proof
> Confronted him with self-comparisons.[9]

It is he who meets Macbeth and Banquo on the heath and brings Macbeth the news that he is the thane of Cawdor. In him too there is no trace of jealousy or envy, he is truly glad that Macbeth has been honoured. He serves the useful purpose of informing him of it. In fact, it is his function to serve some useful purpose in the play, usually of giving information. In Act IV, sc. ii, it is he to whom the Old man talks and he gives many useful pieces of information. It is a scene in which we have supernatural portents other than those concerned with the witches. The Old Man tells of a hawk and an owl and Ross adds his own bit:

And Duncan's horses...
Turn'd wild in nature, broke their stalls, flung out.[10]

After this Macduff comes and they exchange bits of new. Actually, the news is imparted by Macduff and Ross elicits the information. His function here is to acquaint the audience with the current affairs.

It is remarkable in the Banquet scene that he is the only lord who speaks. The rest of the guests do not say anything. He has the courage to ask Macbeth the question "What sights, my lord?" and earlier it is he who remarks that Macbeth is not well.

In the awful scene in which Macduff's family is attacked and killed it is Ross who comes to warn her. He is her cousin and senses that she is in danger.

But cruel are the times when we are traitors
And do not know ourselves.[11]

After warning her he goes. It is significant that he should say that we do not know who are traitors. It means that he does not know for sure whom to suspect, but he does not think that either the grooms or Malcolm and Donalbain killed Duncan.

He comes to England to meet Macduff and Malcolm. He knows what has happened to Macduff's family but does not tell him at first. A bit later he realizes that hiding the truth will be no good and he tells Macduff in a brutally straightforward manner.

Your castle is surpris'd; your wife and babes
Savagely slaughter'd.[12]

His patriotism is evoked on seeing them and he exclaims:

Alas poor country
Almost afraid to know itself. It cannot
Be call'd our mother, but our grave.[13]

His brutal and straightforward manner in talking to Macduff is most unexpected. But he does it deliberately, so as to arouse his anger, not to overwhelm him with sorrow and he is definitely successful in doing so. Before long Macduff is seething with vengeful ire. He does not try to console Macduff as Malcolm does.

It can be seen that though a minor character he serves several functions, usually that of giving information, to the characters as well as to the audience. But he has got a certain individuality of his own, as indeed all of Shakespeare's characters have.

A Scotch Doctor

This is the Doctor who attends to Lady Macbeth. We see him first in Act IV, sc. i. He is talking to the Gentlewoman who attends to her. They have been watching Lady Macbeth for two nights but for these two nights she had been quiet and had not walked in her sleep. But it is his duty to attend to her and he is not going to give up. So this is the third night that he is watching her. His perseverance is rewarded. Lady Macbeth enters with a lighted candle and at once he asks "How came she by that light?" If she is asleep then it is quite possible that she may set the house on fire if she carries a lighted candle. But she does not do so. Instead she speaks and the Doctor notes it down:

> Hark, she speaks. I will set down what comes from her, to satisfy my remembrance the more strongly.[14]

As she talks and he observes, he makes comments on her and finally says:

> This disease is beyond my practice: yet I've known those which have walked in their sleep, who have died holily in their beds.[15]

But then he has seen habitual sleep-walkers, not one who is driven to walk in her sleep because she is impelled by a guilty conscience. He realizes this, and, being an astute man, realizes far more:

> Foul whisperings are abroad: unnatural deeds
> Do breed unnatural troubles; infectious minds
> To their deaf pillows will discharge their secrets:
> More needs she the divine than the physician:
> God, god forgive us all.[16]

In other words, now he knows everything, or almost everything. Not only he, but others also.

We see him next in V: iii where he tells Macbeth about Lady Macbeth's illness. He tells him that her disease is a mental one:

Not so sick, my lord
As she is troubled with thick-coming fancies
That keep her from her rest.[17]

Not a very enlightening report, but Macbeth understands it all right for in answer comes the famous question: "Canst thou not minister to a mind diseas'd?", etc.

It is to him that Shakespeare gives the honour of ending the scene with a soliloquy of a couplet:

Were I from Dunsinane away and clear,
Profit again should hardly draw me here.[18]

The Doctor, true to his calling, is a good and efficient physician and knows his limits full well. He is also dignified, for he does not fawn upon Macbeth. Here is another highly individualistic well-drawn minor character.

A Sergeant

Such a very minor character would not have been considered ordinarily. But the Sergeant in Macbeth is a special case. He is present in only one scene, and not the whole of it, only the first forty lines. But he speaks most of these 40 lines and most eloquently, except for Duncan interjecting. This is how he describes the battle and it should be remembered that it is an eye-witness account by a soldier:

Doubtful it stood
As two spent swimmers that do cling together
And choke their art. The merciless Macdonwald—
Worthy to be a rebel for to that
The multiplying villainies of nature
Do swarm upon him....
For brave Macbeth—well he deserves that name—
Disdaining fortune, with his brandish'd steel
Which smoked with bloody execution
Like valour's minion carv'd out his passage...
And fixed his head upon our battlements.

Then again he says to Duncan's question "Dismay'd not this?"

Yes
As sparrows eagles or the hare the lion...
Except they meant to bathe in reckless wounds
....
Or memorize another Golgotha
I cannot tell:[19]

After this he goes out, never to be seen again, but he leaves his mark on the audience. All the lines he speaks have not been quoted, but most of them have been.

It has been already remarked that this eloquence of the Sergeant has been frowned upon by many critics. According to Aristotle and also others, particularly Horace, characters should speak according to their age, sex, and station in life. The Sergeant definitely does not conform to this rule. Shakespeare has given him poetry of a high order, as is usually given to noble characters. This is an error of judgement on our poet's part, and has been duly condemned. But it cannot be denied that he has given us another unforgettable, highly individual character.

Porter

The Porter of the famous Porter Scene also, like the Sergeant speaks a few lines in a much longer scene. The scene has already been discussed in Chap. 4 (*vide* Chap. 4, discussion of II: ii *supra*). It remains for us to take a closer look at his character.

He speaks only a few lines of prose which in different editions are different in number, not even high-class poetry as the Sergeant does but he is a highly humorous man and provides the only example of comic relief in the play. Macduff and Lennox have come and they are knocking for admittance. The porter hears them knocking and does not open the gate. This happens thrice. After he has heard the knocking for the fourth time he finally opens the gate.

He is a highly fanciful man and he pretends to himself that he is the porter to the gates of hell and every time he hears the knocking he pretends that a sinner who is dead is knocking for admittance. He does not open the gate but he talks to this hypothetical sinner in a joking manner. The first time he hears the knocking he pretends it is a farmer who had hoarded a stock of grain at low price, hoping to make a huge profit when the price went up. But the price did not go up and so he hanged himself:

> Here is a farmer that hang'd himself
> o'th' expectation of plenty: come in time,
> have napkins enow about you here; you
> will sweat for it.[20]

He tells the farmer to have plenty of napkins because the place is hell and therefore very hot. He will need plenty of napkins because he will sweat a lot. He jokes with each one in a like manner.

The second time he hears the knocking he imagines it is an equivocator, i.e. a fraud who makes his living by cheating others,—a double dealer:

> Faith, here is an equivocator that could
> swear in both the scales 'gainst either scale
> who committed treason enough for God's
> sake, yet could not equivocate to Heaven:
> ho come in equivocator.[21]

Next, for the third time, he imagines it is a tailor who has cheated his customer:

> Faith, here is an English tailor come
> hither for stealing out of a French hose:
> come in too, here you may roast your goods.[22]

Then he hears the knocking for the fourth time and decides it is time that he opened. So he opens the door, but with a parting shot for the audience:

> I pray you, remember the porter.[23]

He is indeed remembered by posterity as has been pointed out in the discussion. He is a humorous character, highly individualized. But this was not realized for a long time till De Quincey's famous essay was published. There is no other porter anywhere like him. He is unique.

Lady Macduff

Lady Macduff is seen in only one scene but in that scene she is a living presence. Though she is not a very forceful character, she is a fully feminine one and such is the impression she leaves. Like all normal wives she is critical of her husband. She is angry with him for having fled the country, leaving them all in danger:

> Wisdom? to leave his wife, to leave his babes
> His mansion and his titles in a place
> From which himself does fly? He loves us not.[23]

Then come the unforgettable lines:

> For the poor wren
> (The most diminutive of birds) will fight
> Her young ones in nest, against the owl.[24]

Ross warns her of danger but she does not yet realize how near the danger is. She is too angry with her husband and talks to her son who is but a child. After some time a messenger comes who warns them to flee the place.

Now Lady Macduff realizes her danger but the warning is too late to give her time to flee the place or to prepare otherwise. But before she can do anything at all Macbeth's hired murderers enter and kill the child and pursue her off-stage.

This is the most unforgivable of Macbeth's crimes. She is an inoffensive, totally defenceless woman and he has her killed by hired assassins. She is fully feminine in her reactions. A comparison with the only other female character Lady Macbeth highlights this contrast: just as Lady Macbeth is fully unfeminine, Lady Macduff is entirely feminine.

Besides these a few more characters are there, the most important of whom are the witches but they have been discussed in the relevant scenes and the theme of the supernatural. The other characters are too insignificant for discussion. But it should be remembered that the poet has endowed each of them with individuality and each has his contribution to make. All of them together serve to make the rich kaleidoscopic background against which the somber tragedy is enacted. They are all necessary.

References

1. I: ii: 24.
2. I: iii: 67.

3. I: iv: 19-20.
4. I: vi: 29-30.
5. II: iii: 120.
6. IV: iii: 20-21.
7. IV: iii: 50-51, 61-63, 86-90.
8. IV: iii: 115-17.
9. I: ii: 54-55.
10. III: iv: 13-16.
11. IV: ii: 18-19.
12. IV: iii: 199-200.
13. IV: iii: 159-61.
14. V: i: 31-32.
15. V: vii: 63-65.
16. V: i: 70-74.
17. I: iii: 38-40.
18. V: iii: 60-61.
19. I: ii: 18-23.
20. I: iii: 33-41.
21. II: ii.
22. *Ibid.*
23. *Ibid.*
24. *Ibid.*

8

The Plot or Dramatic Technique

According to Aristotle there are six elements of tragedy and he lists plot as the first of them. It is "the soul of tragedy" and the most important of all the elements. No less than nine chapters are devoted to it and many are the rules given by him. The Elizabethans knew them quite well and some of the basic ideas will be explained now.

(A) THE CLASSICAL RULES

First of all it is necessary to know that definition of tragedy as given by Aristotle in his *Poetics*:

> Tragedy then, is the imitation of an action that is serious, complete and of a given magnitude; in language embellished with each kind of artificial ornaments, the several kinds being found in separate parts of the play; in the form of action, not of narration, through pity and fear affecting the proper purgation of these emotions.[1]

Later commentators have argued endlessly about virtually every word of this definition and added corollaries and interpretations. It is not necessary to know about them. Let us take up the most obvious rules about the play. They are rules of the unities. There are three unities and many of the side issues have been added by later commentators. They are:

(1) the Unity of Action

(2) The Unity of Time

(3) the Unity of Place

However strictly the critics talk about them the dramatists themselves take many liberties with them. Specially, Shakespeare treats them quite cavalierly, sometimes observing them, sometimes not. Ben Jonson is the only one who observes them carefully and he writes satirical comedies, not tragedies. It should always be remembered that the rules apply to all plays, not just tragedies.

(1) THE UNITY OF ACTION

This is the most important of the Three Unities, direct reference to it is in the definition when Aristotle says "an action that is serious, complete in itself and of a certain magnitude". This, among other things, has two implications: (a) the plot of a tragedy must be serious, i.e. without any comic scenes, incidents, etc. Any inclusion of comic scenes will be a violation of the rule. (b) There must be only one action, i.e., no sub-plots. Most of the Elizabethan tragedies flout these rules, Shakespeare is among them. Even then, the present play comes nearest to observing these rules. There is only one speech pertaining to comic relief and though there are many intrigues there is no sub-plot as such. Ben Jonson again observes this rule faithfully. Intrigues there are many in his plays, but no sub-plots.

(2) THE UNITY OF TIME

On the face of it, this should be the most difficult of all the unities. It implies, at least according to the neo-classicists, that the time covered by the play should be the performance time on the stage. That is, if it is three hours' acting time on the stage, the actual time of the play must be only three hours. This is an ideal impossible to achieve. Aristotle, knowing this, had extended the time limit to one day, "a single revolution of the sun". Even this might seem to be impossible but actually Ben Jonson's plays take one day for their actual time. As for Shakespeare and more particularly the present play, the time covered is 17 years, from the death of Duncan to the death of Macbeth (*vide* Chap. 3, *supra*). The Greek plays, of course, followed this rule. The acting time of *Oedipus* is the same as the actual time. Ben Jonson allows himself a full day, from dawn to dusk, in his plays.

(3) THE UNITY OF PLACE

This means that the play should take place in one place only, without a change of scene. This is manifestly impossible. Even

Ben Jonson allows himself different rooms in a house, sometimes the adjoining garden. Elizabethan plays of course played havoc with this unity also, especially Shakespeare. In the present play of course he goes to England, let alone many other places.

Let it be observed that when Shakespeare wanted to, he could observe the unities all right. *The Tempest* is a case in point. All the unities have been observed in it. The most flagrant flouting of the unities can also be observed in him.

The most famous defence of Shakespeare from this point of view is the one given by Dr. Johnson. He is referring specially to the unity of place in the sentence given below:

> The truth is that the spectators are always in their senses and know from the first act to the last that the stage is only a stage and the players only players....[2]

In other words, if the audience can imagine the theatre hall to represent the streets of Athens then he can imagine the same stage to represent the wood in which Oberon and Puck fly about (*M.N.D.*). The same can be said about the other unities. The Elizabethan audience, though thoroughly credulous, had a highly flexible and adaptable imagination. A little flouting of the unities did not matter to them. They were, unlike scholars, after the entertainment. They were ready, in Coleridge's words, to willingly suspend their disbelief.

Many commentators have expanded Aristotle's theories. One of the most famous is Donatus and his treatise was widely read by the Elizabethans. He is the one who has divided the plot into five parts, starting with the Prologue. In *Macbeth*, the first scene is the Prologue. Shakespeare has also written Prologues separately but usually it is incorporated within the first scene or the first Act.

Donatus has given us a five-fold structure of a tragedy which is the one that came to be followed by the dramatists. In fact, they had to study the treatise as part of their courses of study. They knew it by heart.

(1) **Prologue**—This introduces us to the play, usually the first scene or two. Marlowe's *Dr. Faustus* contains a Prologue in the classical manner.

(2) **Protasis**—The action begins. The characters are introduced.

(3) **Epitasis**—Summa epitasis or catastasis—this is the main body of the play. The summa epitasis is the climax.

(4) **Catastrophe**—The winding up of the action. In tragedies usually the death of the hero, which it need not necessarily be. Oedipus does not die.

(5) **Epilogue**—Comments on the action. Marlowe's *Dr. Faustus* has got a classical epilogue. In Elizabethan plays, it is usually the last speech which shows the restoration of moral order.

Certain other classical terms concerned with the plot have to be explained now. *Peripeteia* and *Anagnorisis* are two terms which are indispenible . Peripeteia means Reversal of fortune, the fall of the hero from a high to a low status. In Sophocles' *Oedipus Rex*, Oedipus is a king in the beginning and at the end he is a blind beggar. In the present case, Macbeth is a great warrior in the beginning and at the end he is a hunted creature. Without peripeteia there cannot be a tragedy. Anagnorisis means Recognition. This can be of many types. At the most superficial level it means the recognition of two characters who had been separated long ago, of each other. This happens in *Twelfth Night* where Viola and Sebastian had been separated through shipwreck and at the end of the play recognize each other. The most subtle recognition occurs when a character recognizes himself. Again the best example is *Oedipus* in which, setting out to find out the cause of the plague in his kingdom, Oedipus finds that he himself is the culprit. In Shakespeare, it occurs again and again when in their soliloquies the characters realize their own natures. In him not even soliloquies are needed for self-recognition. The character, in an aside (in the presence of others) can recognize his own failings or strength, as is the case here, with Macbeth's asides.

Aristotle has also told us what the ideal plot for tragedy should be. He gives three kinds of plots that tragedy must not be and then gives the ideal plot. He explores all the possibilities:

(a) a good man coming to a bad end—moving but not moral.

(b) a bad man coming to a good end—not a tragedy at all

(c) a bad man coming to a bad end—moral, but not moving

(d) a rather good man coming to a bad end—both moving and moral, it is ideal for tragedy.

It is while explaining this last kind that he talks of "hamartia" and peripeteia. A complex tragedy involves peripeteia. Besides these tragedies contain Pathos or Scenes of Suffering, to be found again and again in Shakespeare. In the present play, the murder-scene of Lady Macduff and her son can be called such. The Sleep-Walking Scene might easily have become one but instead it is awe-inspiring. As Bradley has remarked it can be called the catastrophe of Lady Macbeth but also observes that "she is too great to repent".

Besides this he classifies tragedy into four kinds, of which the complex is the best, involving peripeteia. *Macbeth* needless to say is a very good complex tragedy.

Conflict is another important concept propagated by Aristotle. It is not that he talks about or lays down rules about it. But it has been developed out of his theories. It was actually Hegel who, inspired by Aristotle formed the theory of conflict and realized that Aristotle's theories do not apply very well to Shakespearean tragedies. He formulated the theory of conflict to apply to tragedies in general, including those of Shakespeare. Bradley arrives at the conclusion that:

> whatever forces act in human spirit, whether good or evil, whether personal passion or impersonal principle; doubts, desires, scruples, ideas—whatever can animate, shake, possess and drive a man's soul. In a Shakespearean tragedy some such forces are shown in conflict.... Treasonous ambition in Macbeth collides with loyalty and patriotism in Macduff and Malcolm.[3]

But this is not enough. Shakespeare is far more subtle. The bitterest conflict in *Macbeth* is a mental one, as will be seen a short while later. It is always so in our poet. The conflict in the outer world is as nothing in comparison with the conflict in the inner world of the mind.

(B) CERTAIN ELIZABETHAN FEATURES

There are many elements in Elizabethan plays that are recognized as being typically Elizabethan. Apart from the

Elizabethan mentality, this applies to the technical aspect of writing plays as well. There are many dramatic devices used at that time. The dramatists followed the classical rules particularly as explained by Donatus, but most of the time modified them so that they became recognized as Elizabethan features. One of them was the matter of sub-plots. This was typical of nearly all Elizabethan plays, whether tragic or comic. It was only Ben Jonson who staunchly kept to the Aristotelian rules as regarding sub-plots.

There must, according to Aristotle, be just one plot in a tragedy. The sub-plot, in violation of his rules, is usually common. This is not the case with *Macbeth*. Here there are intrigues that are subjugated to the main plot but no sub-plots. The student should know that the sub-plots were related to the main plot in many different ways but there is no need to study them because the topic has nothing to do with our play.

Another well-known feature of the Elizabethan play is the presence of the supernatural element. It is present in this play from the very beginning. Aristotle calls it "the marvelous" and approves its presence:

> The marvelous should be represented in tragedy.... The marvelous is a source of pleasure.[4]

He regards it as "pleasure-giving" because so it is in Greek plays. But in Elizabethan plays they are used for this purpose (as in *M.N.D.*) as well as to inspire awe and fear as in *Macbeth*. In this play, the supernatural elements are present in direct contradiction of the Aristotelian dictum. He also says in a famous rule:

> Probable impossibilities are to be preferred to improbable possibilities.[5]

Elizabethans believed in ghosts, fairies, and witches. They had these two guidelines to follow and developed their own theories. There were many contemporary books dealing with supernatural phenomena: Reginald Scot's *Discovery of Witchcraft* (1584), Burton's *Anatomy of Melancholy* and Lavator's *Of Ghosts and Sprites Walking by Nyght*.

This topic has been extensively discussed in the preceding chapter especially under the topic of theme (*vide* Chap. 5 *supra*). There is no need to explain it again. With reference to Aristotle's remark that they are pleasure-giving it has to be remembered that in *Macbeth* they certainly are not and with relation to the later remark about probable impossibilities it is to be remarked that to the Elizabethans the witches were neither improbable nor impossible. The Elizabethans regarded them as real, though extraordinary. In the Chronological Table of the events of Shakespeare's time (*vide* Ch. 1: Background) it has been remarked that the last recorded witch-burning was as late as 1612, four years before our poet's death. So all this was real enough. It is historically true, not just hearsay.

Another feature of Elizabethan plays were the soliloquies. They reveal the speaker's inmost thoughts, when he is alone on the stage. The soliloquies in *Macbeth* are not so important as those in *Hamlet* but on the other hand one of them reveals the presence of supernatural elements independent of witches: "Is this a dagger", etc. As it is critics regard even the asides (spoken in the presence of other characters) in this play as soliloquies but the last two are quite important, specially the one revealing Macbeth's reflections on life as being a tale told by an idiot, signifying nothing. This will be discussed later in this chapter.

There are many other features of Elizabethan plays like the dumb-show, the play-within-the-play, the masque, etc. that serve to provide entertainment and lighten the atmosphere. They have been repeatedly used in other plays, but not in this. This has served to intensify the atmosphere of gloom and horror in it. Not for nothing is the play known as the darkest tragedy. If no lightening or entertaining or beautifying device is used such an effect is inevitable. *Hamlet* is a most somber tragedy whose appeal is mostly to the intellect. But there are many such devices used in it for lightening the solemnity like the Ghost, the dumb-show, the play-within-the-play. They have all been used in it and none of them is there in *Macbeth*.

The use of comic relief is another typical Elizabethan feature. This has followed from the tradition of the native English mediaeval plays according to modern research. It has been frowned upon by the neo-classical critics but it is solidly based upon tradition. The Porter Scene in this play provides this comic relief. This has also been discussed twice (*vide* scene-wise analysis and the character of the Porter *supra*) so there is no need to repeat it. Let it be remembered that for however short a time the scene provides comic relief and lightens the atmosphere. De Quincey, as has been said already, regards the Porter Scene as a stroke of genius, signifying the return of ordinary life.

(C) THE PLOT OF *MACBETH*

If we take the classical rules and analyse *Macbeth* according to them it will be seen that most of them have been violated. In Act I itself there are so many changes of scenes, flouting the unity of place:

Sc. i – A desert place.
Sc. ii – A camp near Forres.
Sc. iii – A heath.
Sc. iv – Forres, the palace.
Sc. v – Inverness, Macbeth's castle.
Sc. vi – Before Macbeth's castle.
Sc. vii – Macbeth's castle.

Here almost every scene is located in a different place. Unity of place is definitely violated. Moreover, this is only one Act. This kind of frequent change of scene takes place in every Act, the worst occurring in Act IV, sc. iii where he goes to England, a different country altogether. Dr. Johnson's masterly defence of Shakespeare's violation of the unity of place has already been quoted in the foregoing pages. It cannot be bettered.

As for the unity of time, the time covered by the play is fully 17 years, as has been pointed out in Chap. 3. There in section (b) a detailed analysis of the time covered has already been given. The action takes nine days and covers the span of 17 years from 1040 the year of Duncan's death to 1057, the year of Macbeth's death.

The only unity that has been almost wholly observed is the unity of action. First of all there is only one action, without any sub-plots. Secondly, there are no scenes of comic relief expecting the Porter Scene which is a small part of a much longer scene.

Following Donatus's division, the plot can arranged in the manner given below:

Prologue	–	Act I, sc. i
Protasis	–	Act I: Macbeth's victory and temptation
Epitasis	–	Act II: Macbeth's hesitation to commit murder overcome and Duncan's murder. Act III: His apparent success, Banquo's murder, Fleance's escape. Act IV: Murder of Macduff's family. Macbeth's decline. This is the Summa Epitasis.
Catastrophe	–	Act V: Macbeth's downfall. It may be observed here that Bradley calls the catastrophe of the play an extended one and in this connection refers to the sleep-walking scene:

> The most impressive scene in *Macbeth* after that of Duncan's muder is the sleep-walking scene; and it may be truly, if not literally, be said to show the catastrophe of Lady Macbeth.[6]

This is how Shakespeare has extended the catastrophe.

It is a complex tragedy, involving both *peripeteia* and *anagnorisis*. Peripeteia is definitely there for in the beginning he is everyone's darling, Bellona's bridegroom and for some time his star is in the ascendant: he becomes the king. Then the reversal comes with his first failure, Fleance's flight. Thereafter, his downfall is swift and at the end he is a hunted fugitive in his own kingdom, Macduff calls him a "hell-hound". He has travelled a long way indeed from Bellona's bridegroom to hell-hound.

Anagnorisis or Recognition is there in a refined form. It is in the form of self-recognition, nothing so crude as the recognition of one character by another. The crudest form it has in this play is Lady Macbeth's recognition of the character of her husband.

Yet do I fear thy nature,
It is too full O' the milk of human kindness
To catch the nearest way, thou wouldst be great,
Art not without ambition, but without
The illness should attend it...would not play false
And yet wouldst wrongly win.[7]

As recognition this is subtle enough, but even this seems crude besides the many speeches revealing self-recognition in Macbeth. There are many of them but all pale into insignificance beside the recognition of his guilt in the passage.

Will all great Neptune's ocean wash this blood
Clean from my hand? No, this my hand will rather
The multitudinous seas incarnadine
Making the green one red.[8]

This is self-recognition at its subtlest.

The theory of conflict is the most important of post-Aristotelian theories. As has already been pointed out, Bradley talks about "treasonous ambition" in Macbeth coming into conflict with the loyalty and patriotism of Macduff and Malcolm. But actually the thing goes much deeper. Conflict exists on two levels, the outer and the inner. Outer conflict is there in the battle between Macbeth and Malcolm's army, but a far more subtle inner conflict exists in the hesitation in and vacillation of Macbeth's mind when he is torn by conflict.

Stars, hide your fires
Let not light see my dark and deep desires.[9]

But this is just the beginning. This conflict is there in Macbeth till the very end, even after Duncan's death. No wonder Hazlitt says:

He is the double thrall of his passions and his evil destiny.[10]

There is much more to be said about the plot of *Macbeth*. Different critics have different opinions. Bradley for example says that the plot is divisible into two parts and

the first part of *Macbeth* is greater than the second and in the first half Lady Macbeth not only appears more than

> in the second but exerts the ultimate deciding influence on the act.[11]

Some critics do not like this simple division of the plot into two halves. M.C. Bradbrook for example writes about two kinds of plots:

> Their system of plotting were very simple.
>
> The most popular were the cumulative and that based upon peripeteia.[12]

It is noticeable that at this elementary stage itself she distinguishes between the cumulative plot and those based upon peripeteia. The two, thus, are different.

Then she proceeds to explain the cumulative plot:

> In the cumulative plot the same type of incident is repeated again and again in a crescendo and with quickening tempo, up to the catastrophe.... *Macbeth* is the supreme example of this kind of plot.[13]

Then she writes about the plots involving peripeteia and it is clear that she is writing about a different kind of plot. But then it is well-known that *Macbeth* is a play with peripeteia in it. Therefore, how are we to reconcile this with the concept of a cumulative plot? Unfortunately, she does not mention this problem, let alone discuss it. She discusses other things.

Dramatic irony is one of the features of Elizabethan plays, which is both classical and Elizabethan, and thus difficult to categorize. Dramatic irony is different from rhetorical irony. The latter occurs when the opposite is said of what is meant. When Antony says "Brutus is an honourable man" he means the opposite. Dramatic irony on the other hand is not limited to speech only and can be said to occur when something significant but nearly the reverse of the expected happens. It can be of many kinds. Apart from verbal irony there are two other main kinds of it.

Verbal irony—This is concerned with words. The most remarkable use of it occurs in Act I. When the witches chant "Fair is foul and foul is fair" it is taken for just a verse chanted by them. There is no irony there. Irony occurs when in sc. iii

Macbeth says: "So fair and foul a day I have not seen." By echoing the witches' words this, thus, at once takes on a different meaning, an ironical significance which had not been there before.

The next most important kind of irony is sophoclean irony. This is found in Sophocles's plays. Bradley explains it thus:

> The speaker is made to use words bearing to the audience, in addition to his own meaning, a further and ominous sense hidden from himself.[14]

The example Bradley takes to illustrate this is the example given for Verbal Irony above, namely Macbeth's opening words. Bradley calls them:

> ...an example to which attention is often being drawn; for they startle the reader by recalling the words of the witches in the first scene.[15]

He gives several other examples. The one from the sleep-walking scene is easily comprehended. In the murder scene Lady Macbeth says: "A little water clears us of this deed" and in the sleep-walking scene all the perfumes of Arabia do not sweeten her little hand. There are dozens of such examples throughout the play.

Retrospective Irony is a phrase used by Quiller-couch. According to him, this Irony comes with the spectator's memory of what has gone before. He gives the example of Macbeth washing his hands and talking of Neptune's ocean. Then Lady Macbeth says "A little water clears us of this deed." The significance of this becomes clear in the Sleep-Walking Scene when the spectator remembers all that had gone before.

There are many other instances of irony called by different critics by different names: Irony of Fate (Moulton), Extended Irony (Bradley), Irony in description, Reminiscent Irony (Quiller-couch), etc. Bradley firmly declares that *Macbeth* is extremely rich in the use of irony.

A word should be said here about the soliloquies. This is an Elizabethan device to reveal a character's thoughts. Technically speaking, soliloquies are those speeches uttered by a character when he is alone on the stage, not in the presence of other characters. Those addressed to the audience in the presence of other characters are "asides". Sometimes, however, as will be seen later on, the character talks to himself in the presence of others. Such speeches have the spirit of a soliloquy, though technically they are "asides". There are quite a few of them in *Macbeth*.

There are, in all, eight speeches in *Macbeth* some of which are technically "asides" but soliloquies in spirit. The first of them is in I: iii which is actually an "aside" but reveals Macbeth's inmost thoughts and has been called, therefore, a soliloquy:

> Two truths are told
> As happy prologues to the swelling
> Of the imperial theme....[16]

The second is also an "aside" but a soliloquy as well: "Stars hide your fixes", etc. in which he is contemplating murder.[17]

The third is fully a soliloquy in which he is alone on the stage. It is a highly contemplative one in which he wonders about the consequences of murder: "If it were done when it is done", etc.[18]

The fourth is also a proper soliloquy. In it, he sees a dagger which he tries to catch:

> Is this a dagger which I see before me....[19]

The fifth soliloquy occurs in Act III. Here he is wondering how to have a throne that carries no danger with it:

> To be thus is nothing....[20]

The sixth comes in Lady Macbeth's presence while he is thinking of killing Macduff's family.

The last two soliloquies are the most important and the first of them is a true soliloquy, the second uttered in the presence of Seyton. Both of them present his view of life:

> I have lived too long....[21]

The last is the famous one after he gets the news of Lady Macbeth's death:

> To-morrow and to-morrow and to-morrow....[22]

This is a very cursory account of the plot of *Macbeth*: Information about its sources, the time-span and other things has already been given earlier (*vide* Chap. 3(b) *supra*). Many other accounts of the plot exist, here only a few have been given. It is not absolutely necessary to know all the arguments.

References

1. Butcher, *op. cit.*, p. 23.
2. Bradley and Wimsatt, *op. cit.*, p. 311.
3. Bradley, *op. cit.*, p. 12.
4. Dorsch, T.S. ed. and transl., *Classical Literary Criticism*, Penguin Bks., 1975, p. 78.
5. *Ibid.*
6. Bradbrook, M.C., *op. cit.*, 49.
7. I: v: 17-23.
8. II: ii: 61-64.
9. I: iv: 51-52.
10. Hazlitt, *op. cit.*
11. Bradley, *op. cit.*, p. 307.
12. Bradbrook, M.C., *Themes and Conventions in Elizabethan Tragedy*, Cambr. Univ. Press, 1969, p. 41.
13. *Ibid.*
14. Bradley, *op. cit.*, p. 283.
15. *Ibid.*
16. I: iii: 128-42.
17. I: iv: 50-54.
18. I: vi: 1-28.
19. II: i: 32-62.
20. III: i: 48-72.
21. V: iii: 22-28.
22. V: v: 19-28.

9
Imagery in *Macbeth*

A painter can paint pictures and can depict the objects of the outer world with colour, pencil and brush. But a poet cannot paint, he can only describe. Such descriptions are the poet's equivalent of pictures—they are pictures in words or images. A poet uses them to make his poetry more appealing and more effective. Images can be functional and decorative and much more. Shakespeare was a past master at giving images. This aspect of his work has been studied and analysed extensively by modern critics. The development of his imagery, the relationship between his images—all have been minutely observed and noted.

Different critics have given different definitions of images Henri Fluchère's definition is one that covers a great many possibilities:

> Imagery may be defined as a concrete illustration drawn upon by the poet to clarify or embellish the object that he seeks to describe.[1]

This definition looks quite comprehensive but even then it is not comprehensive enough to take in all the complexities of Shakespeare. Here Fluchère talks about clarification and embellishment, but Shakespeare's images do many other works in addition to them. They create a mood, foretell the future, help to clarify a character's mind, etc. In addition, there is another characteristics of images that Fluchère is quick to point out.

Rhetorical figures, imagery and symbols, all these are so intimately related that often they merge easily enough into each other. It becomes difficult to detect, if any, the difference between them. Besides, their original, own characteristics overlap so that the same, identical and one figure of speech can be an image and an undoubted original symbol. That is to say an image can be all three at once. Fluchère, with acute perception, says:

> No strict rule allow, us to say at what point we pass from the plane of pure psychology and even the metaphysical plane, for the use of imagery.[2]

Again, the same image can be categorized under several heads, i.e., a sense image can also be a nature image, a domestic image, etc. First of all then a categorization is necessary. The most basic categorization is on the basis of the senses. There are five kinds of sense-images corresponding to our five senses. They are entirely physical there is nothing spiritual, intellectual or emotional about them. These values are alien to them. They are:

> Visual image – those pertaining to the eyes,
> Auditory images – those pertaining to the ear,
> Olfactory images – those pertaining to the nose,
> Gustatory images – those pertaining to the tongue,
> Tactile image – those pertaining to the skin.

There is another phenomenon related specially the sense-images—synaesthesia, which means the mixture of more than one sense image. Needless to say, all of these are to be found in Shakespeare. In fact, it is time to give illustrations from him. As far as possible the images have been taken from the first Act only. Otherwise, it will be difficult to choose—there are so many attractive images scattered throughout the play.

> In thunder lightning or in rain.[3]

Here we have a complex image. As far as the senses are concerned, there are three senses involved here: thunder—auditory, lightning—visual, rain—tactile. It is also nature image and a weather image. We have here three different characteristics merged into one.

> That will be ere the set of sun.[4]

This is a visual image and a nature image. In addition it foretells the future.

Fair is foul and foul is fair:
Hover through the fog and filthy air.[5]

Here we have weather image, tactile and visual image and in "fair is foul", etc. we have a hint of symbols, though their meaning is not clear yet. But they definitely create the dark and gloomy mood, full of mystery and fear, that is basic to the play.

As two spent swimmers that do cling together
And choke their art.[6]

Here the image is that of swimming, that is, a sporting image and also a visual one. There is also the figure of speech simile.

And fortune on his damned quarrel smiling
Showed like a rebel's whore.[7]

The image here is that of a woman of easy virtue, which is a simile also, that is, a figure of speech in addition to an image. It carries an aura of moral disapproval. There is a simile here too.

With his brandish'd steel
Which smoked with bloody execution
Like valour's minion carried out his passion.[8]

"Brandish'd steel" is a visual image, a figure of speech (material for the thing made—synecdoche), and a martial image. "Smoked" etc.—a visual and a martial image. "Like valour's minion"—a simile added to an image of affection as "minion" implies. But it carries an air of moral disapproval as minions were looked upon with disfavour.

As sparrows eagles or the hare the lion.[9]

This is a simile, an animal image and a sporting one. It carries the aura of disdain, since Macbeth is too valiant and brave for his adversaries.

Or to memorise another Golgotha.[10]

The image is a Biblical one and therefore a religious one too. Religious allusion is a figure of speech also.

Till that Bellona's bridegroom....[11]

There is classical allusion here which is a figure of speech in addition to the image of a bridegroom associated with happiness and marriage. It is also a metaphor because Macbeth is being directly called Bellona's bridegroom, and a visual image.

These few examples from the first two scenes of the play, it is hoped, have served to illustrate the complexity and richness of the imagery of *Macbeth*.

There can be images from different branches of knowledge to enrich poetry. Duncan says to Macbeth

> I have begun to plant thee and will labour
> To make thee full and growing.[12]

This is an image from agriculture or gardening as well as a nature image and a visual one. One of the plant images in the play refers to botany or horticulture. But so unobtrusively that the need for knowledge never obtrudes upon the reader. Nor is there any parade of learning.

Again there is the passage by Banquo:

> This guest of summer
> The temple-haunting martlet, does approve,
> By his loved masonry that heaven's breath
> Smells wooingly here.[13]

This long image refers to the temple-haunting bird martin. It is a complex one because in addition to other things it refers to considerable knowledge about the habits of birds, that is, ornithology as a branch of knowledge. Such images from different branches of knowledge serve to enrich poetry and they are scattered throughout the play.

It is but to be expected that Macbeth being a warrior the play should have images about battles and wars. Very early in the play we come across martial images, from most unexpected quarter—the witches. They are the first to give us a martial image:

> When the hurly burly's done
> When the battle's lost and won.[14]

We have another martial image a few lines later, in the next scene in the introduction of the famous sergeant

> This is the sergeant
> Who like a good and hardy soldier, fought
> 'Gainst my captivity.[15]

There are images from ordinary everyday life throughout the play, giving it a touch of ordinary homely life, like "the milk of human kindness" and others. They are not so frequent in *Macbeth* as in other plays, which adds to the mood of darkness in it.

One of the most authentic studies of Shakespeare's imagery has been done by W.H. Clemen who has studied, besides other things, the development of Shakespeare's imagery in his entire career. As his art developed, so did his imagery. The images in the early plays are often used for poetic effect, for the purpose of beautification. But in the later plays, as his art developed they became more functional and mature, serving different functions, like developing the theme, developing character-portrayal, setting the mood, creating the atmosphere, clarifying the motives of a character, foretelling the future, etc.

> The more Shakespeare becomes a conscious dramatist, the more he employs them for dramatic purposes. The images gradually lose their purely "poetic", often extraneous nature and become one of the dramatic elements.[16]

The images of *Macbeth* are very mature ones. His images in it show that he views human characters in a new manner. The passage he chooses to illustrate this point is the famous one in which Macbeth is speaking of Duncan. He is afraid that Duncan's virtues will paint him all the blacken, and he is perfectly right in this:

> his virtues
> Will plead like angels, trumpet-tongued, against
> The deep damnation of his taking-off;
> And pity like a naked new-born babe
> Striding the blast, or heaven's cherubim, horsed
> Upon the sightless courier of the air....[17]

This is one of his famous soliloquies, remarkable for its extraordinary images. Referring to the image of pity Clemen says it:

> may illustrate how far Shakespeare has removed from the conventional type of personification and how far his imagery tends towards the strange and the unique.[18]

He analyses the entire passage, then coming to the last lines he says:

> Thus an image, once set afire, as it were, seizes upon everything still to be said and creates bold and most extraordinary concepts like "vaulting ambition".[19]

Caroline Spurgeon, another authoritative scholar of his imagery, says of this image:

> ...and finally the vision of his "intent", his aim, as a horse lacking sufficient spur to action, which melts into the picture of ambition as a rider vaulting into the saddle with such energy that it "o'erleaps itself" and falls on the further side.[20]

This shows how refined the study of his imagery has become in the hands of serious critic. Spurgeon is a pioneering and highly sophisticated critic. Later critics have followed her with care and devotion.

Again, Clemen refers to Macbeth's words on sleep while he is half out of his mind:

> Methought I heard a voice cry "sleep no more!
> Macbeth doth murder sleep", the innocent sleep.[21]

Clemen points out that the series of metaphors describing sleep are very different from those he wrote earlier. In the other plays very often they are ornamental. Here they reveal the character's mental condition.

> ...the imagery of this passage is of the greatest dramatic suitability. For sleep in this case is no "theme of conversation" but a dramatic issue of the first importance. The rich imagery is no digression.... Macbeth perceives

> again and again what he has done with a strange clarity and explains this in imagery.[22]

Caroline Spurgeon talks about "iterative imagery" which helps create the prevailing atmosphere of a play. These images recur throughout the play and the whole play has to be studied with this in mind. In *Macbeth,* images of darkness and gloom are spread throughout the play, creating its prevailing atmosphere. As Bradley says:

> Darkness, we may even say blackness, broods over this tragedy.[23]

As has already been printed out (*vide* Chap. 5, sec. b, *supra*), Bradley elaborates this point, giving numerous quotations from the text on the images of gloom and horror. Besides this, other critics have pointed out many supporting facts such as there are nineteen scenes of darkness and only seven of dusk. All this is the result of its imagery, as given by Caroline Spurgeon. A few quotations from different parts of the play will clarify the point.

(a) When shall we meet again
In thunder lightning or in rain?[24a]

This is from the very first scene of the play and it definitely creates the atmosphere.

(b) Come, thick night
And pall thee in the dunnest smoke of hell.[24b]

This comes towards the end of Act I and reinforces the gloom of the play.

(c) The night has been unruly
Where we lay our Chimneys were bloom down
And (as they say) lamenting heard i' th' air
Strange screams of death.[24c]

This is from Act II, the middle of it.

(d) by the clock 'tis day,
And yet dark night strangles the travelling lamp.
It is night's predominance or the day's shame
That darkness does the face of earth entomb.[24d]

This is from Act III, that is, the middle of the play but by repeating unnatural portents it strengthens the unnatural atmosphere.

Besides these, images of death and disease abound in the play, culminating in the famous question put by Macbeth to the Doctor attending Lady Macbeth:

> Canst thou not minister to a mind diseas'd,
> Pluck from the memory a rooted sorrow,
> Raze out written troubles of the brain.[25]

Clemen has given a very important idea of imagery, that of "imagery-consciousness". Here imagery becomes so much a part of the poet's consciousness that instead of rising to the surface it lies hidden and one has to guess at it:

> The whole image has sunk below the surface, as it were, and left behind it only one or two ideas concerned with it. From Shakespeare's middle period on we have frequently been forced to ask what image did Shakespeare have in mind?[26]

By the time Macbeth has planned the killing of Macduff his thoughts are so full of murder that he does not have to use the word and Lady Macbeth understands it without its being spoken.

> I am in blood
> Steeped in so far that should I wade no more
> Returning were as tedious as to go o'er
> Strange thoughts I have in head, will to hand
> Which must be acted, ere they may be scann'd.[27]

Here the idea of killing has not been mentioned even once, but it is understood all right. It is the underlying image of murder that is working here. Besides this there are many other instances of imagery-consciousness in *Macbeth*, but this is the most effective as it is easily understood by the audience.

"Image-complex" is another term given by Caroline Spurgeon. It means a tendency to bring certain different things together. This is how Clemen explains it:

> The term "image-complex" is to indicate that Shakespeare in his images shows, as Miss Spurgeon has put it, a predilection for "certain classes of things, certain qualities in things and certain aspects of life."[28]

Let us take a passage which will amply illustrate this idea of "image-complex" in *Macbeth*. It is the famous soliloquy uttered by Macbeth when he receives the news of Lady Macbeth's death. Here there is the idea of the passage of time the uselessness of time, the uselessness of life, all brought together in a climatic passage:

> To-morrow and to-morror and to-morrow
> creeps in this petty pace from day to day
> To the last syllable of recorded time...
> ...it is a tale
> Told by an idiot, full of sound and fury
> Signifying nothing.[29]

Here first of all we have the idea of time fleeting by and being recorded. Then there is the idea of everything being useless even fleeting time, of torchlight leading us to death, of life being like a candle to be blown out at a breath, of life being totally meaningless. This basic idea is illustrated with a quick succession of seven images, all signifying in their own way the meaninglessness of life. This is what "image complex" means. There is here a wealth of different images, brought together to illustrate the idea, and supremely successful at that, for no one will deny that his is one of the most effective passages in the whole of Shakespeare.

It will now be seen, in a detailed analysis of one passage how the points given above can be clarified in one passage. As many of the points mentioned will be covered as are relevant. The passage is the famous one uttered by Macbeth after he has killed Duncan. He is washing his hands and he fancies that not only will his hands never be clean, but, in a magnificent and terrifying outburst of imagination, thinks that it will make the sea itself red:

> Will all great Neptune's ocean was this blood
> Clean from my hand? No, this my hand will rather

The Multitudinous seas incarnadine
Making the green one red.[30]

First of all there is the concept of sense images. In this passage, we have visual ("this blood"), tactile ("wash this my hand will rather"), visual again ("Making the green one red"). There is no synaesthesia here but we have four images in quick succession. There is the domestic image of washing too, quite homely.

All these, in addition to being sense images, are also nature images and elemental ones because they are from the element of water. The figure of speech Rhetorical Question and hyperbole are also involved because the first two lines make up a rhetorical question. The next three lines about his hands reddening the ocean are hyperbolical. Here we have symbolism also because water is symbolic of life as well as of cleanliness. So we have symbolism, rhetoric and images all blending with each other.

Different branches of knowledge are not involved in this passage but there is one point about this passage that is missed by the students unless pointed out. The line "Making the green one red" can be understood to mean "Making the green one // red", that is, "green one" meaning the ocean. But it actually, or also, mean "Making the green // one red", that is, one whole red. This makes the enormity of his crime even more heinous. The visual implication of the entire sea becoming red makes one shudder specially as the sea is known as "sea-green incorruptible". Macbeth's crime has made even the incorruptible element polluted. It is a really terrifying idea.

W. Clemen pointed out that as his art matured the images became less decorative and more functional. A more functional passage than this can hardly be imagined. The images are not decorative at all, they serve to point out the psychologically pitiable condition of Macbeth and highlight his repentance. It also, as Clemen says "tends towards the strange and the unique" because a stranger concept than a human hand colouring entire oceans can hardly be imagined and its uniqueness is well-known since an idea like this has not been imagined before or since. When the uniqueness of the image has to be admitted it has to be admitted likewise that this very uniqueness deprives it from being what Caroline Spurgeon calls "iterative" image because the effect of that kind of image depends upon its repetition whereas this is not repeated at all. It is used just once.

Clemen's concept of imagery-consciousness can be seen in the passage when we notice that the word "kill" or "murder" has not been used even once. But the reader understands it because it has permeated Macbeth's consciousness, he does not have to use the word.

When we take up the term "image-complex" we have to admit that in this connection only one idea has been talked about, not a set of many ideas. It is a passage with just one meaning.

This account of Shakespeare's imagery in *Macbeth* is a very cursory one but it is hoped that it has given an idea of the richness and complexity of Shakespeare's mature imagery. Many topics in imagery, however, have not been touched as they are not relevant.

References

1. Fluchere, *op. cit.*, p. 167.
2. *Ibid.*
3. I: i: 2.
4. I: i: 5.
5. I: i: 12-13.
6. I: ii: 8-10.
7. I: ii: 15-16.
8. I: ii: 21-23.
9. I: ii: 34.
10. I: ii: 39.
11. I: ii: 53.
12. I: iv: 28-29.
13. I: vi: 3-6.
14. I: i: 3-4.
15. I: ii: 3-5.
16. Clemen, W., *The Development of Shakespeare's Imagery.*, Lond., Methuen, '77 rpt. p. 81.

17. I: vii: 1-27.
18. Clemen, *op. cit.*, p. 98.
19. *Ibid.*, p. 99.
20. Spurgeon, C., *Shakespeare's Imagery*, Cambr. Univ. Press, 1935, p. 335.
21. III: ii: 35-40.
22. Clemen, *op. cit.*, p. 101.
23. Bradley, *op. cit.*, p. 279.
24. (a) I: i: 1-2, (b) I: v: 48-50, (c) II: iii: 36-39, (d) III: iv: 6-9.
25. V: iii: 39-41.
26. Clemen, *op. cit.*, pp. 71-78.
27. III: iv: 136-40.
28. Clemen, *op. cit.*, p. 28.
29. V: v: 19-28.
30. II: ii: 60-63.

10

Poetic Style in *Macbeth*

One of Shakespeare's names is the Bard of Avon which is an indication of his status as a poet. The poetic style of Shakespeare has been studied extensively and intensively. His style is extremely versatile as it reflects his age (of Elizabethan-Jacobean drama) and his individual personality as well. Besides, technically speaking, the style has to suit each speaker and the situation and Shakespeare is right almost every time, except sometimes in the early plays, so marvellous is his sense of style. It is as if he instinctively know what kind of style to choose in a given situation. There is no other dramatist who can fulfill all these requirements except perhaps Ben Jonson. But his scope is limited—satirical comedy, but Shakespeare deals with every kind of drama, a "Johannes factotum" as Greene derisively called him (*vide*, Chap. 2 *supra*).

His plays, according to contemporary custom, used both prose and verse, the noble characters speaking poetry and the humble using prose. In the present play, however, there is one notable exception—Lady Macbeth in the Sleep-Walking scene, while not in her proper senses, speaks prose. But then even noble characters, in extraordinary situations speak prose in other plays also, in Shakespeare's or other's.

Style however has two aspects: diction and versification. In the discussion given below for the sake of convenience, first diction and then versification will be considered, in two separate sections.

(A) POETIC DICTION

From Aristotle onwards, many classical critics have given many rules about poetic diction. The Elizabethans were familiar with all of them and more or less followed them. Horace's ideas are the most clear-cut and the most relevant. In his *Ars Poetica* he gives clear-cut rules to follow. He is strictly of the opinion that

(a) the diction should suit the genre of poetry
(b) the diction should suit the character speaking.

In drama, according to him, the character should speak in accordance with not only their age, sex and status in life, but the situation also. He looks into every possibility:

> It will make a great difference whether a god or a hero is speaking, a man of ripe years or a hot-headed youngster in the pride of youth, a woman of standing or an officious nurse, a roving merchant or a prosperous farmer.[1]

Horace's acumen is admirable for he has taken in different professions and different speakers from all the walks of life. He makes distinctions between:

(a) a god and a hero
(b) a mature man and a young man
(c) woman of standing and an officious nurse
(d) roving merchant and prosperous farmer.

Thus, he covers nearly all possibilities in his own day. The list, of course, can be added to according to the need of the age. It can go on *ad infinitum*. What matters here is the basic idea that the language must suit the speaker and naturally this requires specialized diction. In this connection, M.C. Bradbrook says:

> The specific style for princes, for lovers, for clowns, was fixed.[2]

These are certain things however that the poet had to keep in mind. The diction should not only suit the speaker, it should be such as to appeal to the spectator or the reader. Fluchère says:

> The Elizabethan dramatist's style is, one of impassioned poetic rhetoric, the two functions of which are to persuade and to touch the emotions.[3]

"To persuade and to touch the emotions," these are the primary aims of poetic style (or prose), they have, from time immemorial (from before Plato that is) been considered to be so as a cursory glance at Greek and Latin rhetorical theories will show.

Greek and Latin rhetoricians also unanimously point out the importance of rhetoric. Aristotle even points out in his definition of tragedy:

> in language embellished with each kind of ornament.[4]

Figures of speech, in other words are obligatory, whoever the speaker might be. In Ben Jonson's *The Alchemist,* the characters are the very dregs of society (frauds, prostitutes, etc.) but figures of speech have been used, whether it is Face who is speaking or Sir Epicure Mammon.

English theorists, of course, followed the ancient masters and approved of figures of speech. The most noted of the theorists of the time, Puttenham writes:

> There is nothing so fitte for the poem as to be furnished with all the figures that Rhetoricall and such as doe most beautifie the language with eloquence.[5]

Many other enlightening things have been said by the ancients. Horace's theories are specially well-formulated ones. Whenever necessary, reference to them will be made in the following pages. Shakespeare and the other Elizabethans knew them quite well and used them extensively.

The style of *Macbeth*, like other aspects of it, is mature. Bradley points out:

> ...the diction has in places a huge rugged grandeur which degenerates here and there into tumidity.[6]

Unfortunately, Bradley's remark on the style of *Macbeth* begins and ends with this sentence. He does not explain or discuss it M.C. Bradbrook, writing about conventions of speech, has nothing to say about *Macbeth*, perhaps, because Shakespeare has gone beyond the convention of "patterned speech" in this play. It is Dr. Johnson who has something definite and memorable to say about his style. He remarks on just one aspect of Shakespeare's style and it will be quoted in the proper place. It is a famous observation, but it is about one aspect only, about Shakespeare's fondness for word-play. He has something to say about his style in general also but it is nothing memorable as he lays stress upon comedy and this is irrelevant in the present context.

Many stylistic devices were available to the Elizabethan dramatists. Imagery was one which has already been discussed in the preceding chapter. Symbolism was one which was hardly used in *Macbeth*. There remains Rhetoric which will be discussed now.

There are many figures of speech and only a few of them can be mentioned. The first of them and the most obvious one is the simile and we have one quite early in the play, in the Sergeant's description:

Doubtful it stood
As two spent swimmers, that do cling together
And choke their art.[7]

This is spoken by the Sergeant and is an extremely effective, though a negative simile. The Homeric simile is a variety of simile and a few lines later the same Sergeant uses it:

As whence the sun 'gins his reflection
Shipwrecking storms and direful thunders break;
So from that spring whence comfort seem'd to come
Discomfort swells.[8]

This simile takes four lines, like one of the similes employed by Homer, and it is also in elevated language. It is used in order to give grandeur and majesty in poetry, which it has definitely done here.

Next comes metaphor which is a very important figure of speech and has been much written about. Following Aristotle Demetrius puts Metaphor under the Elevated style and says that well-chosen metaphors give dignity to the style while familiar words are held cheap. Also, directly following Aristotle's *Rhetoric* he says that metaphors should not be crowded together as is the case with dithyrambic poetry. Both Aristotle and Demetrius regard a simile as an extended metaphor. There are very few passages in Shakespeare which can stand beside the famous passage in Act V so far as the matter of metaphor is concerned.

It is the passage by Macbeth spoken when Lady Macbeth is dead and he receives the news:

> To-morrow and to-morrow and to-morrow
> Creeps in this petty pace from day to day
> To the last syllable of recorded time.
> And all our yesterdays have lighted fools
> The way to dusty death: out out brief candle
> Life is but a walking shadow, a poor player
> That struts and frets his hour upon the stage,
> And then is heard no more. It is a tale
> Told by an idiot, full of sound and fury
> Signifying nothing.[9]

This is a passage that cannot be equalled even in Shakespeare, to take only the metaphors; there are seven of them here, in ten tines, each unique. Each can be called a symbol also. Demetrius, writing about the use of metaphors in prose, had this to say:

> Metaphors should not be crowded together, or we shall find ourselves writing dithyrambic poetry in place of prose.[10]

This passage here is blank verse of a very high order, as near Pindaric poetry (dithyrambic) as is possible in English.

To go back to Act I, there is Ross's famous lyrical description of Macbeth:

> Till that Bellona's bridegroom, lapp'd in proof
> Confronted him with self-comparisons.[11]

This classical allusion is apt to be called a personification also but actually it is a metaphor since Macbeth is being directly called Bellona's bridegroom. It is first a metaphor and next a personification. Here three figures of speech have merged into one another till they are inseparable: metaphor, personification and classical allusion. Also, apart from this, is imagery from which point of view it has already been commented upon.

Antithesis is a figure of speech that lends a dramatic quality to poetry and we find it quite early in the play:

First Witch: Lesser than Macbeth, and greater
Second Witch: Not so happy, yet much happier
Third Witch: Thou shalt get kings, though thou be none.[12]

Here we get an example of antithesis which consists of half of a sentence contradicting the other half, as has happened here, with the first half of a sentence contradicting the other.

There are two more such figures that involve contradiction within a sentence. One of them is Chiasmus in which two halves of a sentence contradict each other in the same words, in an inverted manner:

Fair is foul and foul is fair.[13]

Here the two halves of the same sentence are placed crosswise and contradict each other.

Synecdoche is a figure of speech based on association. We get an example of it in Act I. It is the Sergeant describing Macbeth's valour who uses it:

With his brandish'd steel
Which smoked with bloody execution.[14]

Here "brandish'd steel" stands for Macbeth's sword. We have the substitution of the material (steel) for the thing made (sword), which means synecdoche.

These few examples are all from Act I except for the "to-morrow" passage which has been taken to illustrate a particular point. There are many more figures of speech in Act I itself and about the rest of the play it is useless to talk,—there are so many. It is, however, necessary to analyse a famous passages from the point of view of rhetoric so that the richness of the style may become amply clear. Macbeth's first soliloquy is being taken for illustration, not the whole but a part of it:

His virtues
Will plead, like angels, trumpet-tongued against
The deep damnation of his taking off
And pity, like a naked new-born babe
Striding the blast, or heaven's cherubim horsed
Upon the viewless couriers of the air,
Shall blow the horrid deed in every eye

That tears shall drown the wind. I have no spur
To prick the sides of my intent, but only
Vaulting ambition which o'erleaps itself
And falls on the other.[15]

Looked at from the point of view of rhetoric only, first of all it is an Enthymeme which according to Aristotle is like a syllogism. It is the orator's weapon to persuade the hearer and according to him there are several varieties of it. He calls the enthymeme "a sort of syllogism" and admits of two divisions with many subdivisions. This passage is like a long argument in favour of Duncan because it is like several syllogisms rolled into one, one after the other. One of them, for example, goes like this:

Duncan is a virtuous man
His virtues will plead for him
This will make my crime all the more damnable.

It goes on like this. Before these lines too, there are others. So the whole is a series of syllogisms or enthymemes.

Next in these lines themselves is a simile:
Will plead like angels, trumpet-tongu'd.[16a]

His virtues are imagined to be like angels. Again in "Humet-tongu'd" we have another metaphor because angels are imagined as having tongues as loud as trumpets.

And pity like a naked newborn babe
Striding the blast.[16b]

Pity is here pictured to be like a new-born baby—another simile because "like" is there.

Or heaven's cherubim, hors'd.[16c]

Cherubim, the second of the nine kinds of angels is here pictured as a rider, i.e., a metaphor, together with a religious allusion which is itself a figure of speech.

Upon the viewless couriers of the air.[16d]

An example of circumlocution because instead of just saying "wind" he takes seven words to say the same thing.

Shall blow the horrid deed in every eye
That tears shall drown the wind.[16e]

"The deed" is imagined here to be something that can be blown (like leaves, etc.) and tears shall drown the wind is a paradox.

> I have no spur
> To prick the side of my intent, but only
> Vaulting ambition etc.[16f]

The metaphor of a horse is continued in four lines.

Thus, we have in these few lines, which are themselves like several enthymemes put together, simile, another simile, a metaphor, a circumlocution, a metaphor, a metaphor, a paradox, a religious allusion and another metaphor to end up with. A rich collection indeed.

Another passage that ought to be analysed comes a little later. It is the one Macbeth utters when he has killed Duncan, in a splendid rhetorical question:

> Will all great Neptune's ocean wash this blood
> Clean from my hand? No, this my hand will rather
> The multitudinous seas incarnadine
> Making the green one red.[17]

Here we have a rhetorical question. Rhetorical questions do not usually need an answer. But this is a question which has been answered by the poet: "No, this my hand", etc. After that we have a hyperbole. The idea that Macbeth's hand will colour entire oceans is definitely hyperbolical. This passage is an example of how even one figure of speech (Rhetorical Question in this case) can make a passage a memorable and an unequalled one.

(B) VERSIFICATION

Versification and diction together go to make up the poetic style of a poet—they are the two sides of a coin. Shakespeare's versification, like the other aspects of his work, developed with the development of his career—it became more mature and refined as time went on. His plays, like all Elizabethan ones are mixtures of prose and poetry. Poetry will be looked at first.

Elizabethan plays were written in blank verse, i.e. unrhymed iambic pentametres. There are many variations in it: the lines may be end-stopped or not, they may be regular iambic pentametres or not. The passage given below for example is regular iambic pentametre:

> Thăt tend/oň mórt/ăl thoúghts,/uňsex́/m̆e he̍re /
>
> Aňd fill/m̆e, from/the crown/tŏ the toé/, top̆-full /
>
> Ŏf dir/ešt crú/eltý,/m̆ake thick/mỹ blood /
>
> Stŏp up/the acc/ešs aňd páss/age tó/rémorše/[18]

Lady Macbeth's terrifying invocation to the evil spirits is in regular iambic pentametre, except for two anapaests in line no. two and four. It does not have any material turns and twists. It is not that rhymes do not occur at all. They do, but then it stops being blank verse. Rhymed iambic pentametre couplets often occur in plays at the end of scenes or to highlight a certain sentiment or to sum up a particular point, etc. Such couplets are known as Senecan "sentences". Macbeth, for example, driven by Lady Macbeth, takes the decision to murder Duncan and says:

> Away and mock the time with fairest show
> False face must hide what false heart doth know.[19]

Usually such sentences occur at the end of a scene, but not always. In *Macbeth* however they usually occur at the end.

Very often, to add flexibility to blank verse, one line is broken up between two or more speakers. Given below is such an example from our play. This technique is known as "stichomythia":

> Malcolm: With my confined harms.
>
> Macduff: Not in the legions
> Of horrid hell can come a devil more damn'd
> In evils, to top Macbeth
>
> Malcolm: I grant him bloody.[20]

The passage given above has stichomythia twice in three lines. The first is in the line broken up between Malcolm and Macduff and a line later again the two together make up one line. This makes for variety and flexibility.

Besides blank verse and couplets *Macbeth* uses another verse form also which is not at all common. It has become possible in *Macbeth* because of the witches. They are extraordinary characters and therefore speak in an extraordinary manner too. Whenever they are present they speak in short tetrametre couplets. So also does their goddess Hecate.

When shall we three meet again
In thunder lightning or in rain?
When the hurly burly's done
When the battle's lost and won.[21]

Again, in Act III, sc. v Hecate speaks:

I am for th' air; this night I'll spend
Up to a dismal and a fatal end
Great business must be wrought ere noon
Upon the corner of the moon.[22]

These couplets are usually iambic tetrametres or trochaic tetrametres. Shakespeare uses both.

Songs are not usual in tragedies, though in some tragedies there are songs as in *Hamlet*. *Macbeth* however does not have any. This does but add to the atmosphere of gloom and horror in it.

A few words should be said about his use of prose in *Macbeth*. In other works, it would not have been necessary but here it is because two of the most famous scenes in it are written in prose: the Porter scene and the Sleep-Walking scene. Both have been studied in the preceding pages, so extensive comments are not needed but a few remarks about prose will be appropriate.

The Porter scene comes first. Here prose is aptly used because it is a low-class character speaking and prose is the appropriate medium. It is equally aptly used in the Sleep-Walking scene because here Lady Macbeth is not in a normal state of mind at all. In fact, the very fact that she is talking in prose is in itself a pointer that she is mentally in an unstable condition, may be not yet quite mad, but on the way to it.

Demetrius divides prose style into four categories: elevated, elegant, plain and forcible, and it is the plain style which is used in this incomparable scene. Aristotle says in this context:

> A writer must disguise his art and give the impression of speaking naturally and not artificially. Nature is persuasive, art is the contrary.[23]

Following this, Demetrius also praises simplicity and he knows that deep and sincere feelings need no ornaments. The Sleep-Walking scene would, all the same; have taxed his ingenuity, for here no style but the Plain is suitable which must be natural and yet convey an impression of unnaturalness or mental instability. Shakespeare masterfully solves the problem by making Lady Macbeth re-live the night of the murder. Even his use of hyperbole is justified:

> Here's the smell of blood still: all the perfumes of Arabia will not sweeten this little hand. Oh! Oh! Oh![24]

This is Lady Macbeth's equivalent of Macbeth's image of Neptune's ocean. Macbeth was in his senses and Lady Macbeth is not. That is what makes the prose even more persuasive and the simplicity more terrifying than if the passage had been in Shakespeare's best poetic vein. This is far more effective, this disjointed prose, than any poetry could have been.

It can be seen, therefore, that in *Macbeth* whatever medium the poet chooses, poetry or prose, he is a master at it. There is ordinary blank verse, tetrametre couplets and prose, all employed just as they should be. *Macbeth* is a product of Shakespeare's mature art as even this aspect of it shows.

References

1. Dorsch, T.S., *op. cit.*, p. 83.
2. Bradley, *op. cit,* p. 45.
3. Fluchère, *op. cit.*, p. 152.
4. Butcher, *op. cit.*, p. 23.
5. Quoted in *ibid.*, p. 189.
6. Bradley, *op. cit.*, p. 278.
7. I: ii: 8-10.
8. I: ii: 25-28.

9. V: v: 19-28.
10. Quoted in Rhys, Roberts W., *Greek Rhetoric*. New York, Cooper Square Pubs. Inc., 1963, p. 164.
11. I: ii: 54-56.
12. I: i: 65-67.
13. I: i: 9-10.
14. I: ii: 18-19.
15. I: vii: 18-27.
16. (a), (b), (c), (d), (e), (f)—all I: vii: 18-27.
17. II: ii: 60-63.
18. I: v: 39.
19. I: vii: 79-80.
20. IV: ii: 55-57.
21. I: i: 1-4.
22. III: v: 21-24.
23. W. Roberts transl. *Aristotle's Rhetoric*, O.U.P., 1924, iii C2.
24. V: i: 47-50.

11
Critical Reception of *Macbeth*

Macbeth has from the very beginning, been acknowledged as one of the poet's masterpieces. It was written in King James's honour, he being a Scottish king like Macbeth. In his own time, it was an accredited masterpiece and the same view has continued up till now. Even the neo-classical critics did not have much to object to as the most important of the unities, the unity of action, has been observed.

The most important work on *Macbeth* in the eighteenth century was Dr. Johnson's *Preface* to it. He remarked on the grandeur of conception but complained about characterization:

> This play is deservedly celebrated for the propriety of its fictions and solemnity and grandeur and variety of its action, but it has no discrimination of characters.... Lady Macbeth is merely detested.[1]

Many critics do not agree with the last statement. In fact, Bradley uses the word "sublime" for her.

The most remarkable essay in the nineteenth century was De Quincey's *On the Knocking at the Gate in Macbeth* which has already been commented upon and quoted from. Before the publication of this essay the Porter scene had been looked upon with derision. Coleridge dismissed it as an interpolation:

> ...the disgusting passage by the Porter (II: iii)
>
> which I dare pledge myself to demonstrate to be an interpolation of the actors.[2]

But the attitude changed at once as soon as De Quincey's essay was published. It presents a completely different view of the play, presenting what had appeared to be a weakness as one of the notable excellences. It is in this connection that De Quincey wrote the famous apostrophe:

> O mighty poet! Thy works were not as those of other men, simply and merely great works of art, but were also like the phenomenon of nature like the sun and the sea and the stars and the flowers.[3]

It is surprising that it was *Macbeth*, the tragedy of gloom and horror that inspired this lyrical outburst.

In the twentieth century, the most authoritative work on *Macbeth* is that of Bradley. His critical method has been called "Romantic expansionist interpretation" and his exposition of the play concentrates on its being a tragedy of gloom and horror but with sublimity in it. We look at:

> ...Lady Macbeth in awe because though she is dreadful she is also sublime. The whole tragedy is sublime.[4]

After a few years, specially after the First World War criticism on Shakespeare became specialized and different critics wrote on different aspects of the plays, like imagery, structure, etc. All these critics acknowledge that *Macbeth* is a masterpiece and speculate on different aspects of it.

The later years, specially those after the Second World War saw the mushrooming of dozens of critical theories and those of the critics who wrote on Shakespeare interpreted his plays according to their theories.

In more recent years inter-disciplinary criticism has come into vogue and in India the latest such attempt is to analyse Shakespeare from the point of view of ancient Sanskrit theories. Of late such a study, analyzing *Macbeth* and other plays from the point of view of the *Rasa* theory has been published. An abridged version of this study is given below. Sanskrit slokas have not been quoted, only phrases and words. Long words have been split up with hyphens. Translations have been given where needed.

Shakespeare in the Light of Rasa-Vāda (by the present writer)

It is said that *Macbeth* is the darkest of Shakespeare's tragedies. We know that Indian poetics does not take favourable view of tragedy. Now let us see what the theory of *Rasa* has to say about it.

Right in the beginning of the play we are taken by surprise because of the supernatural element and this element is scattered throughout the play. We see a heath with three witches in it. They talk in couplets, not in blank verse. They decide that later on in the same day they will gather together in the same place, after the battle is over, to meet Macbeth. Then they depart, after chanting the famous couplet "Fair is foul", etc.

The *rasa* we get here is *adbhuta-rasa* which has surprise or *vismaya* as its permanent emotion (*sthāyībhāva*): *vismayātma raso-adbhuta*.

The main ingredient of this *rasa* is *camatkāra* (the marvellous). Āchārya Kṣemendra has given ten kinds of poetic *camatkāra* (*Kāvya-gata daśavidha camatkāra*). We get the *camatkāra* of the *avicārita-ramaṇīya* kind here for the scene does not need intellectual effort at all in order to appreciate it. There is another *camatkāra* besides this: *samasta-sūkta-vyāpī camatkāra*. The conversation of the witches raises wonder: how did they know that a battle will be fought, how do they know about Macbeth, etc. Very few first scenes are there that offer so much to marvel at, i.e. the element of *camatkāra*.

In sc. ii, Duncan gets the news of the battle from the Sergeant. He is not an important character but the poet has given him poetry of a high order:

> As when the sun 'gins his reflections
>
> ....
>
> Doubly redoubled Strokes upon the foe.[5]

Here *adbhuta* is generated along with *vīra-rasa*. The speech of the Sergeant is the *Uddīpana* (excitant), Macbeth, though absent, is the *ālambana* (semblance), the king and the others the *āśraya* (recipient). Macbeth is a *yuddha-vīra* (warrior), so we get *vīra-rasa* as well. The *adbhuta* we get here is based on joy, *ānandaja* not *divya* (divine). There is no *rasa-virodha* (conflict of the *rasas*) because *adbhuta* does not conflict with any *rasa*, it can peacefully co-exist with all the *rasas*—*savatra-api-rasah-adbhuta*.

After this Ross comes. No *rasas* are generated here. There are many *sancārī bhāvas* (transitory emotions) but they do not last for long enough to condense into *rasas*.

The scene after this is on the heath and the three witches are there. After some time Macbeth and Banquo come. There is thc gradual creation of *adbhuta rasa*. It gets built up slowly but surely. The witches greet him. The seed of trouble is sown by the third witch who says he "shall be the king hereafter", then they greet Banquo and prophesy to him. Up till now both of them, awestruck, had been silent. As soon as Macbeth asks them how they know all this, they vanish.

We definitely get *divya-adbhuta* here. The witches are the *ālambana* (semblance), their prophecies and appearance are the *uddīpana* (excitant). Macbeth and Banquo are the *āśraya* (recipient). The *camatkāra* we get is of the *avicarita ramaṇīya* kind. The *rasa* is generated (*utpatti*) slowly and is nourished (*puṣti*) and is successful (*niṣpatti*) while the witches are on the stage.

After this scene again things change. There are many *bhāvas*, mainly *vismaya*, but no rasa, nor in the next scene. Creation of *rasas* is no easy matter. It takes time and trouble to create *rasa*, then do we get that experience which is known as *lokottara-camatkāra-prāṇa,* i.e. that which makes us marvel at that which transcends the ordinary world.

We see Lady Macbeth for the first time in the next scene (I: iv). She is the main, almost the only, female character (except for Lady Macduff) in the play but not the heroine in the usual sense, definitely not like the heroines of Sanskrit poetics. She reads Macbeth's letter and she understands his ambition soon enough:

Hie thee hither
That I may pour my spirits in thine ear.[6]

Here too it is *adbhuta* that we get, because her reactions are not ordinary, they provoke surprise. Along with this we get two kinds of *camatkāra*. The first of them is *vicāraymāna ramanīya* because her analysis of his character surprises us and the second is *samasta-sūktaryāpī ramaṇīya* because the full soliloquy, in its entirety, surprises us. We realize that this is no ordinary woman.

Along with a strong personality she has a firmness of character and great ambition. We shall gradually understand how unique a personality she is.

The soliloquy after this strikes us with awe. She invokes the evil spirits:

> Come you spirit
> That tend on mortal thoughts, unsex me here
> ....
> That my keen knife see not the wound it makes.[7]

Here the gentle murmur of *adbhuta* is drowned by *udvegībībhatsa.* This rasa is not easy to come by. It is generated by mental disgust. We see that this lady's mind is not as that of any other woman, nor of any ordinary man. It is mental disgust that generates *vdvegī bībhatsa* while simple *bībhatsa* is only physical disgust. We also experience mental disgust at her invocation of evil spirits. It is generated slowly (*utpatti*) establishes itself firmly (*pūṣti*) and then subsides (*niṣpatti*). It is there along with *adbhuta* but far stronger. Again, after a slight interval it is generated again as she talks to Macbeth, telling him to act like a loyal and grateful subject, advising him to

> look like the innocent flower
> But be the serpent under it.[8]

The disgust we feel has not been born from the senses but is of our intellect. The scholars Ramachandra-Gunachandra and following them the modern scholar Dr. Nagendra had talked about it.

In the next scene, Duncan comes to Macbeth's castle. Here for a short time we have *Prakṛti rasa.* It is not one established by the ancients but by the moderns. Here nature herself is the *ālambana*, not the *uddīpana.* This scene is the only one where there is no darkness and horror. The description given by Duncan and Banquo transfers us, for however short a time, into a different world where there is no rebellion, no treachery, no hypocrisy. The "temple-haunting martlet" generates *prakṛti.* The palace itself, the bird, etc. are the *ālambana* and the king and the other are the *āśraya* of this *rasa. Prakṛti* or *udatta* was thought of by Bhoja then it was firmly declared to be a *rasa* by the Hindi scholar Ramchandra Shukla.

The next scene contains the famous soliloquy "If it were done", etc. This soliloquy offers *vicāryamāna ramaṇīya* for a long time. There are not many instances of such a long exposition of this kind of *camatkāra*. Some of the soliloquies of *Hamlet* are like this and the famous degree speech of Ulysses in *Troilus and Cressida*. Some relevant lines are being given below:

...that but this blow,
Might be the be-all and the end-all here,
But here upon the bank and shoal of time
We would jump the life to come...
...this even-handed justice
commends the ingredients of our poison'd chalice
To our own lips...
And pity, like a naked new-born babe
Striding the blast, or heaven's cherubim horsed
Upon the viewless couriers of the air
Shall blow the horrid deed in every eye
That tears shall drown the wind.[9]

This passage definitely gives us the experience that *rasa* alone can give. The question is, which *rasa*? The problem is that none of the well-known *rasas* seem to be apt. We do get the *camatkāra* of the *vicāryamāna ramaṇīya* kind but that is not the property of *adbhuta* alone.

We shall have to turn to modern scholars. Mr. Vide talks about *Udvega* as a *rasa*. The fear, sorrow, anxiety, etc. we experience when we see corruption in the powerful class of society is called *udvega rasa*. Mr. Vide does not talk about the other points of the *rasa*-experience, the *sthāyi*, the *uddīpana*, etc. at all in a systematic manner but from the little he says this seems to be the *rasa* here.

We next experience *rasa* in the dagger speech. It is a hallucination that Macbeth sees but all the same it generates *adbhuta*. Macbeth is the *āśraya* and the dagger the *ālambana*. The presence of the king, his own ambition, Lady Macbeth's prodding—all serve as *uddīpana*. This is the *rasa* that has *utpatti, puṣṭi* and *niṣpatti* in this entire speech. The *rasa* is *divya adbhuta* since a supernatural phenomenon is concerned. In this play, we get this variety of *rasa* again and again but every time it is created by something evil. This is quite a rare phenomenon.

Macbeth's speech while washing his hands is poetry of a very high order and so also is the *rasa*-experience. Here indeed do we get the feeling that this is the *Lokottara-camatkāra prāṇa* experience that *rasa* alone can offer. The feeling of guilt and self-condemnation has almost driven him mad. We get two types of *bhayānaka* here. *Trāsa* (fear) is the *sthāyī* of this *rasa*, the god presiding over it is Yama and the colour is black. There are three kinds of *bhayānaka*: *kṛttrim* (artificial), *aparadha-janya* (guilty consciousness) and *bitrāsita* (fear). We get the last two here. The hero is conscious of his guilt. He is afraid that he will never be forgiven for his crime. His crime has polluted the whole world. Duncan, dead, is the *ālambana*, the act of murder is the *uddīpana* and Macbeth the *āśraya*. *Rasa* has received *utpatti*, *puṣṭi* and *nāṣpatti* extremely neatly.

The Porter scene offers us *hāsya rasa*. Ācārya Dhananjaya has analysed this *rasa* extremely competently, dividing it into six kinds and assigning each to different kinds of characters. Here in the Porter's speech we get *upahasita hāsya*. In this kind of *hāsya,* the head shakes with laughter: *sa-śira-kampamidam upahasitam*. This is meant for the characters of *madhyama* (middle) type. The Porter is not a character of this type but of a lower type so the laughter should have been of the *apahasita* or the *atihasita* type but laughter of that degree is hardly ever to be found in Shakespeare. Here also, the laughter is controlled. The Porter himself in laughing so the laughter is *ātmastha*. The knocking is the *uddīpana* and the dead souls he imagines to be waiting outside are the *ālambana*. Actually, it is Macduff and Lennox who are waiting and knocking. But they are not the *ālampana*, instead imaginary, non-existent characters are. This is extraordinary—the actual characters are present yet imaginary characters are type *ālambana*.

Then with the discovery of the murder everything changes. For a very short time, just a few lines, we get *rasa*-experience. It takes time for the entire *rasa*-experience to take place, its *utpatti*, *puṣṭi* and *niṣpatti*. But our dramatist's power is so wonderful that he can create *rasa* even for a very short time:

Macduff : O horror, horror
Tongue nor heart cannot conceive nor horror name thee
Macbeth and Lennox : What is the matter?
Macduff : Confusion now hath made his masterpiece:
Most sacrilegious murder hath broken ope
The Lord's anointed temple.[10]

Though for short time, *vitrāsita bhayānaka* is generated. The dead body of the king is the *ālambana*, the news of his murder is the *uddīpana* and all except Macbeth are the *āśraya*. Macbeth is not because he knows very well all that has happened and just pretends to be shocked. After that no *rasas* are generated.

The next scene gives us *adbhuta* again because many supernatural things happen. Darkness at noon and a falcon killed by an owl, etc. It is *divya adbhuta* with Ross and the Old Man as the *āśraya*.

We get *Māyārasa* in a small speech of Lady Macbeth in III: ii. She is thoroughly disillusioned and says:

Nought is had, all is spent
Where our desire is got without content
'Tis safer to be that which we destroy
Than by destroying dwell in doubtful joy.[11]

Here is *māyārasa* receiving generating (*utpatti*), nourished (*puṣṭi*) and subsiding (*niṣpatti*) very effectively. Lady Macbeth realizes that all their efforts have led to nothing. The crown and the throne has brought them nothing. Everything is useless. This is the main idea behind *mithyā-jñana*. Bhanudatta says that *mithyā-jñana* is the *sthāyī* of *māyārasa*. We shall get *māyārasa* even more firmly established when Macbeth enters. His speech also gives *puṣṭi* to *māyārasa*. The guilt and self-condemnation due to murdering the king is the *uddīpana*. This is the speech with the lines:

Duncan is in his grave
After life's fitful fever he sleeps well

Such is Macbeth's state of mind that he envies the one he has killed. The husband and wife are standing on a heap of ashes. *Mithyā-jñana* condenses into *māyārasa*.

Again when he tells Lady Macbeth about killing Banquo and says, highlighting the darkness of the play:

Good things of day begin to droop and drowse
When night's black agents to their preys do rouse.[12]

Here also we find *māyārasa* being continued. This scene is the nourisher of *māyārasa* for with slight intervals it occurs again and again.

In this stopping and recurring so many times of the same *rasa* the *rasa-bighna* of *paunah punyena dīpanam* kind cannot be said to have occurred, because it is not that every time the *rasa* is created anew. Rather, with more of intensity or less the same *rasa* is continued. Husband and wife, both are sick with self-disgust and disgust at the world. What better conditions for *māyārasa* can there be? For *rasa-bighna* of *paunah-punyena dīpanam* kind interruption is needed. Here there is no interruption but rather a continuation.

In the Banquet scene, Macbeth comes to know that Banquo is dead so for the time being he is free and *prakṛti* is generated. Bharatendu Harishchandra who established this *rasa*, had said it is created by the serenity that is produced in our mind when contemplating nature's beauty. He does not say how to regard it if dissatisfactory emotions are felt. The lines definitely create *rasa*:

There the green serpent lies, the worm that's fled
Hath nature that in time will venom breed
No teeth for th' presents.[13]

Rasa is definitely experienced here, but which *rasa*? Not *bībhatsa* because there is no disgust here, nor *bhayānaka*. *Prakṛti* is suitable here. Banquo's death is the *uddīpana*. Here we can say that the seventh kind of *camatkāra* given by Kṣemendra—*śabdārthagata camatkāra* is what we get here. Before this we have seen *camatkāra* associated with *adbhuta* but it is not limited to that *rasa* only. This is *kavya-gata daśavidha camatkāra* (ten kinds of the marvelous in poetry) and can exist anywhere. Macbeth is the *āśraya*, the imaginary snake the *ālambana*. *Rasa niṣpatti* has happened very effectively, though limited to three lines only.

We get both *bhayānaka* and *adbhuta* in the Banquet scene. *Atilaukika padārtha* is there in the Ghost and Macbeth himself acknowledges that he is afraid of it. Here we get two kinds of *bhayānaka*, *aparādha-janya* and *vitràsita*. Macbeth is *āśraya* of both. It has already been said that the *adbhuta* occurring in this play is not a pleasant one and here it is mixed with *bhayānaka* and this will happen repeatedly.

....

Now for the other things concerned with the play. First comes the question: What is the *aṅgī-rasa* (the main *rasa*) of this play? This is a tragedy so *karuṇa* should be the *aṅgī* of this play, but that does not happen. Even at the end, when *karuṇa* reigns supreme in other tragedies, it does not gain any prominence here. We do not see the death of the hero or that of the heroine either. Let us now think of the three characteristics of the *aṅgī*. These are *vahuvyāpti, pātrodyama* (the hero's effort) and *phalāgama* (the result). It will be seen that according to the first, *adbhuta* is the *aṅgī*. No other *rasa* has been generated as many times as it has. Seven of the scenes have only *adbhuta* (I: i, I: iii, II: iv, III: iv, III: v, IV: i, V: i). Besides these it is present in many others also. So the condition of *vahuvyāpti* is fulfilled.

The second requirement is *pātrodyama* (the hero's efforts) also is there because right after the three prophecies the hero devotes himself to killing Duncan and the others, thus bringing about the tragic end.

As far as *phalāgama* is concerned, our play is a little weak on this issue. But if we remember that it is the prophecy of the witches that have been ultimately fulfilled then again *adbhuta* is successful.

As a hero, Macbeth is definitely a *dhīroddhata* one, because he is a *yuddha-vīra* (warrior). All the characteristics of such a hero, pride, hypocrisy, etc. are there in him. Jealousy, anger and self-satisfaction are lacking, but he is *a dhir-oddhata nāyaka* all right.

Lady Macbeth is not a problem just for the *rasa* theorist only, but for all critics. She is unique, no one can reach her. But if one has to she can be categorized as a *svīyā, jyeṣṭhā* and *madhyā-adhīrā* character. The last of them chides her husband again and again as she does. What a strong character hers is! It is a pity that everything turned towards evil and that is why she is Lady Macbeth, towering over every Elizabethan heroine.

References

1. Bratchell, *op. cit.,* p. 133.
2. *Ibid.*, p. 138.
3. *Ibid.*, p. 142.
4. Bradley, *op. cit.*, p. 227.
5. I: ii: 25-37.
6. I: iv: 23-26.
7. I: v: 31-50.
8. I: v: 62-64.
9. I: vii: 2-25.
10. II: iii: 45-49.
11. III: ii: 5-8.
12. III: ii: 51-52.
13. III: iii: 29-31.

Some Important Questions on *Macbeth*

1. Discuss *Macbeth* as a "tragedy of gloom and horror".
2. "The whole tragedy is sublime." Do you agree? Give reasons for your answer.
3. Analyse *Macbeth* as a Conqueror Tragedy.
4. "Macbeth grows into evil." Is this a true evaluation of his character? Give reasons for your answer.
5. "Though she is terrible she is also sublime." Analyse Lady Macbeth's character in the light of this remark.
6. Analyse the plot of *Macbeth*. OR Give an account of the dramatic strategies used in *Macbeth*.
7. Write a note on the imagery of *Macbeth*.
8. Analyse the Porter scene in the light of Comic Relief.
9. Write a note on the Banquet scene in *Macbeth*.
10. Analyse the Sleep-walking scene in *Macbeth*.
11. Discuss the element of the supernatural in *Macbeth*. OR Analyse the part played by the Weird Sisters.
12. Write a note on the poetic style of Macbeth.

A Select Bibliography

Bayley, John, *Shakespeare and Tragedy*. London, Routledge and Kegan Paul, 1981.

Bradbrook, M.C., *Themes and Conventions in Elizabethan Tragedy*. Cambr. Univ. Press, 1935.

Bradley, A.C., *Shakespearean Tragedy*. London, Routledge, 1960.

Bratchell, D.F. (ed.), *Shakespearean Tragedy*. Lond., Routledge, 1990.

Campbell, Lily B., *Shakespeare's Tragic Heroes*. Cambr. Univ. Press, 1930.

Clemen, W., *The Development of Shakespeare's Imagery*. London, Methuen, 1951.

Ellis-Fermor, U., *The Jacobean Drama*. Lond., Methuen, 1960.

Leech, Clifford, *Shakespeare's Tragedy*, Lond., Chatto and Windus, 1950.

Schelling, F.E., *English Drama*. Delhi, S. Chand & Co., 1963.

Spencer, T., *Shakespeare and the Nature of Man*. New York, The Macmillan Company, 1945.

Ornstein, R., *The Moral Vision of Jacobean Tragedy*. Univ. of Wisconsin Press, 1960.